DAVID N. EBNER

STUDIO
FURNITURE

DAVID N. EBNER

STUDIO FURNITURE

Nancy N. Schiffer

Schiffer Publishing Ltd

4880 Lower Valley Road • Atglen, PA 19310

Other Schiffer Books on Related Subjects:
Studio Furniture from Today's Leading Woodworkers, Tina Skinner, ISBN: 978-0-7643-3287-6, $39.99
Mind & Hand: Contemporary Studio Furniture, The Furniture Society, ISBN: 978-0-7643-4115-1, $29.99
Craft Furniture: The Legacy of the Human Hand, Dennis Blankemeyer, ISBN: 0-7643-0496-5, $59.95
Esherick, Maloof and Nakashima: Homes of the Master Wood Artists,
Stephen Whitsitt & Tina Skinner, ISBN: 978-0-7843-3202-9, $49.99

Copyright © 2013 by Schiffer Publishing

Library of Congress Control Number: 2013950795

Photos are by Gill and Stephen Amiaga or David Ebner, unless otherwise noted.

Designed by John P. Cheek
Cover design by Danielle Farmer
Type set in Abadi MT Condensed / Adobe Jenson Pro

ISBN: 978-0-7643-4414-5
Printed in China

Published by Schiffer Publishing, Ltd.
4880 Lower Valley Road
Atglen, PA 19310
Phone: (610) 593-1777; Fax: (610) 593-2002
E-mail: Info@schifferbooks.com

For the largest selection of fine reference books on this and related subjects, please visit our website at **www.schifferbooks.com.** You may also write for a free catalog.

This book may be purchased from the publisher.
Please try your bookstore first.

We are always looking for people to write books on new and related subjects. If you have an idea for a book, please contact us at
proposals@schifferbooks.com.

Schiffer Books are available at special discounts for bulk purchases for sales promotions or premiums. Special editions, including personalized covers, corporate imprints, and excerpts can be created in large quantities for special needs. For more information contact the publisher.

CONTENTS

FOREWORD

The first time that I had the opportunity to see David Ebner's work in person was at the SOFA art show in New York in 2001. He was set up in space exclusively devoted to his work that was so visually appealing that it was impossible not to pay attention. I was immediately drawn to what was clearly one of the most original designer/makers working in the United States. As I was specializing in vintage work from Wharton Esherick, George Nakashima, Sam Maloof, and others, the appeal was totally visceral with no consideration of handling this contemporary work. However, I recognized that Ebner was on the same level as these other classic, established designers. What really impressed me was that his work was not derivative at all, but combined the various influences of those who preceded him in a manner that was all David Ebner.

As fate would have it, the gallery that was carrying David's work at the SOFA New York show chose not to do the show in 2004. I jumped at the opportunity and reconsidered my commitment to vintage work, at least as regarded David. I asked him if I could represent him at SOFA New York. This began what has been a long-term relationship for us. Until now, he has been the only contemporary woodworker I have represented, and I am very proud of it.

It is exciting to represent David's work as he is constantly developing his ideas and designs in fascinating ways. He forged a style of his own from the very beginning and has never allowed himself to stop evolving. He is always thinking, designing, and making new work that advances his aesthetic growth and pushes the envelope of contemporary design. Further, the craftsmanship is at such a high level that it will always be appreciated for its skill and quality. His work is the best of the best—the most creative and innovative of the third generation of American woodworkers.

I am so very pleased that Schiffer Publishing has recognized David's importance in the Studio Furniture Movement and has chosen to publish a book about him and his furniture. David's work is work for the future. The designs will always be classic and likely influence generations to come.

Robert Aibel
Moderne Gallery
Philadelphia, Pennsylvania

Interior of a Brookhaven Hamlet residence with furniture made by David Ebner, 1998.

PREFACE

The Mission

I want to convey something about my initial mission and what I wanted to focus on, if I were going to devote the majority of my working life to making furniture. From day one, I wanted to produce a major body of work, in numbers as well as in diversity. Early on, I started with the idea that I didn't want to be known for one particular style, not that there's anything wrong with that; it just wasn't the way I wanted to go about it. Through the years, I've constantly made changes, just to keep interested or avoid copying myself. Growth was always very important, as was longevity. We used to joke about it, but you don't want to end up thirty years later repairing everything you made in the first thirty years. Luckily, we've only seen one or two pieces come back for repair from use or abuse. It is easy to take a few liberties that down the line will shorten the life of the piece.

I have a punch from Richard Scott Newman, one of the premier furniture makers through the 1980s, who also came out of R.I.T. (Rochester Institute of Technology). He always felt that you don't make something if it's not sound, which I thought was a rather lofty ideal, because you could research every adhesive and every attachment. In principle, though, I like that idea. You want people two hundred years from now to be able to walk into a home or a museum and see how I applied a part. I always felt that you learn from history to make history, and it continues. The people who look at my work will take the next step in another direction; I've always been conscious of that. This is how I would cover the basics of what I'm thinking about as my mission.

The Approach

My approach to making a piece hasn't changed dramatically over the years. I still go through the same steps, from napkin sketch to full-scale mechanical drawing to construction. My ideas can come from sculpture, architecture, or furniture, and that mix has stayed pretty constant. My thoughts about function have also remained the same. Some of the forms may be more abstract and the materials more unusual, but they still produce functional furniture. A bench of my twisted-stick furniture can look like pure sculpture, especially if it is ebonized or finished with graphited lacquer, but in the end it is still a bench.

Other things have changed, though. When I started out as a designer, I sometimes explored classic periods of furniture; I would look at Chinese, Japanese, or Colonial designs, pare them down to the bare roots, and make furniture in that mode. I don't do that any more. There are almost no period references in my current work. My inspirations tend to be more abstract. I might look at Chinese calligraphy and develop furniture forms from the simple, beautiful lines of those brush strokes.

My stamina and attention span today aren't what they were. I used to be able to put my head down and just go; when I looked up it was fifteen hours later. Today, after a couple of hours, I find myself needing to look at other things. So, I don't work those huge blocks of time on one specific thing. But at this point, I have made 1400 pieces; I have the luxury of working very intuitively. I trust my own eye much more and I can look at something and come up with a solution almost immediately. If I belabored the decision and spent two weeks worrying, I would probably wind up with the same solution.

I see fewer new faces in the field than I did years ago, fewer energized, committed, young makers. I'm not sure what has caused this, but it seems that the idea of embracing the whole process of making rather than just the result doesn't hold much appeal any more.

Or maybe it's the economy. I know I have felt the downturn very significantly. It is certainly not the 1980s anymore; I now have one full-time and one part-time assistant. In the late 1980s, I had three full-time assistants and two part-time ones, and we were all young and energetic and working like hell. It wasn't a matter of "Where is the work coming from?" It was, "What is the next due date?" Today it is piece-to-piece. A friend recently reminded me that I have been through this three or four times in the past. And it's true: there have been ups and downs in the field before. But when I was young, the bumps in the economy didn't matter because I could live on much less. Now I need to turn a bigger nut, so the economics are a challenge.

Despite the struggles, I am grateful I still have some place to go every day and something I want to do. I wound up making furniture because I enjoyed the whole process—from concept to drawing to engineering to fabricating to working with clients—and I still do. And I have a whole tent full of wood waiting to be used.

David N. Ebner, 2013

ACKNOWLEDGMENTS

I was quickly drawn to the elegance of furniture designs I found in David Ebner's work, when the idea of producing this book first evolved. His exquisite craftsmanship was immediately apparent and his unusual choice of materials seemed original and interesting. I had to learn more. David Ebner's natural enthusiasm for his work has been infectious, making this book a delight to research and compile. He has been most gracious in our interviews and provided catalogs, books, photographs, and ideas in abundance.

Most importantly, David thanks his parents for the lifetime of support and encouragement, and in particular his mother, who still does his books. This wonder journey would not have happened without them.

Right away, Robert Aibel, owner/director of the Moderne Gallery in Philadelphia, was quick to ask how he could be helpful, and he was. His Foreword explains his respect for David and his work, and the confidence he feels in its importance to American studio arts.

Stephen Amiaga, of Amiaga Photographers, Inc., provided a majority of the images that document this furniture, which he and his father have produced throughout David's career. Also, LuAnn Thompson, from Bellport Arts & Framing Studio, was helpful in preparing many of the images that are included here.

We thank all the galleries that have supported David's work and the studio furniture movement: encouragement from Jack Lenor Larson; Elaine Benson Gallery, Bridgehampton, New York; Gallery North, Setaucket, New York; Gallery Henoch, New York City, through the encouragement of Joseph Reboli; W. Zimmer Gallery, Mendocino, California; Robert Aibel, Moderne Gallery, Philadelphia; and Bebe & Warren Johnson, Pritam & Eames Gallery, East Hampton, New York.

We thank all the studio helpers through the years; without their commitment and expertise, the body of pieces would not have been possible: Al Roe, who has been with David from the beginning; Wane Zimerman; Jeffery U.; Raphial Addams; Gerhard Redelberger; Russel Ebner (no relation); and many others. Jody Brown rode shot-gun on all those long road trips in David's patched-together, overloaded, delivery vans.

Doug Congdon-Martin's keen editorial and technical abilities have helped to direct the book's final phase. Each person's effort is gratefully appreciated

Chapter 1
GETTING STARTED
1945–1972

Oil on canvas portrait of *David N. Ebner,*
c. 1975, by New York City pulp illustrator and
Catholic holy card artist, Raphael DeSoto,
from Puerto Rico.

David N. Ebner was born in 1945 and grew up near Buffalo, New York, spending considerable time in his father's basement workshop. He once told Chris Cromeyn that he always knew he would work in and with wood.

> "My first big success [was] the baseball bats I made for Little League." At age nine, he made his own baseball bat using his father's lathe and later worked on boats, pipe organs and antique furniture, just to be working with wood, his favorite material for expression. "I look at it as a material that is also a medium," said Ebner.
>
> "Bellport artisan on…The Cutting Edge," *The Long Island Advance*, June 3, 1999, page 11

Jonathan Binzin tells the story of an eight year-old Ebner encountering a Frank Lloyd Wright house in Buffalo, New York, as he left a Cub Scout meeting:

> It baffled him, and he became fascinated with Wright and with all sorts of architecture and engineering. Buildings and bridges continue to inspire him, and many of his furniture designs, he says, are "architectural statements in a furniture format."
>
> *Seats of New York: Benches, Stools, & Chairs from Across the State,* June 19–July 17, 2008, Purchase, New York: Richard & Dolly Maass Gallery, Purchase College, SUNY, 2008, page 20

In a 1991 exhibition catalog, John Perreault recalls Ebner saying, "If it had anything to do with wood, I kept myself involved, to build my vocabulary."

> He may start with a design idea and then look for the proper wood, or find some wood that suggests a design idea, but wood is central. Although he may quote the past, his love of the medium saves him from post modernist ironies. He thinks in wood and it shows.
>
> "Explorations II, The New Furniture," New York City: The American Craft Museum, 1991, page 16

David Ebner was encouraged by his Kenmore East High School woodworking teacher, Ken Hodge, who wrote two special courses for him to get a Regents sequence, so he could apply to the Rochester Institute of Technology (R.I.T.).

Ebner remembers:

> The man who taught me Woodworking 101, and then all through high school, Mr. Hodge, was the head of Industrial Arts Woodworking program for the Regents for New York State. He wrote *Woodworking 3 and 4*, which had never existed as courses, into a Regents program, so I could have four years of woodworking in high school. Every study hall and every time between soccer practice he opened the woodworking shop to me, even on weekends. He really pushed for me, expanded the opportunities early on. I learned my early techniques in craftsmanship from him.

With this background, Ebner was well-prepared when he entered R.I.T. Maxine Rosenberg reports that "his ability to construct well-made furniture placed him far ahead of most other students." (*Artists of Handcrafted Furniture at Work.* New York: Lothrop, Lee & Shepard Books, page 21.)

At the Rochester Institute of Technology, Ebner was accepted into the School of American Craftsmen in 1964. He studied under instructors Wendell Castle and William Keyser, who taught there. At the School for American Craftsmen, Ebner realized there was an "artistic approach" to the woodworking that had consumed him while growing up. He remembers:

> I'd always been fascinated by the Frank Lloyd Wright houses in Buffalo and loved to visit the Albright-Knox Art Gallery there, but never thought of myself as a potential artist-craftsman in wood.

Ebner's *Chest of Drawers*, in mahogany was the first organic piece of furniture he made, as a college sophomore, at the Rochester Institute of Technology, in 1965. It demonstrates the influence of Wendell Castle, in designing organic furniture. Ebner still makes the form on occasion. This was the inspiration for the *Lingerie Chest* that David Ebner made twenty years later.

His B.F.A. Thesis Exhibit furniture was made in 1968. Drawings show a matching chair and desk, the *Receptionist's Desk*, and the *Coffee Table* of rosewood and paint.

Ebner's first lathe-turned piece, *Bowl,* walnut and maple, made in 1960, during his freshman year in high school. 10.5" d x 3" h.

Chest of Drawers, 1965, shown outdoors just after it was completed. Photo by William Apton.

Chest of Drawers, mahogany, 1965.
This was David's first venture into organic furniture. He wanted it to be part of a tree, with the branches coming out of the trunk.

David Ebner's first vacuum-formed *Occasional Chair* was made in 1965, while he was a student at Rochester Institute of Technology, with technical assistance from R.I.T. Professor Bill Keyser. Photo by William Apton.

Tulip-shaped chair of bent wood with upholstered cushion seat, vacuum-formed, made at R.I.T., c. 1967.

Telephone stand, 1965, oak pedestal, made for a project involving a telephone. It was made with a drawer at R.I.T. and has the first, hand-cut dovetails that David Ebner made.

Blanket Chest, cherry, with hinged lids and interior compartments, leather straps and handles, 1965.

Game Table, walnut and contrasting leather checkerboard, with two storage compartments underneath, 20"d x 18"w x 30"h, 1966. Ebner remembers:

> That's a chess table or game table, with storage underneath in a small compartment. That's in walnut and leather. It has the first through joints I ever made, an exercise at R.I.T. One of the things I did as a student, although not always embraced by the faculty at R.I.T., we had to do five different pieces each year, it could be a chair, easy-chair, desk, whatever. I always chose to use different techniques for each piece; I really wanted to learn as many techniques as I could. They [the faculty] felt you should just design something and then whatever technique you needed to make it, you would do it. I always threw myself into it well; I'll design something, but I'm going to design it with a technique in mind because I just wanted to explore as many different techniques as a student while I was there.

Easy Chair and *ottoman* with cushions, wood frame and upholstered back and seat, 36" h x 32" w x 28" d. This was among Ebner's student work at R.I.T., 1966.

Dining Chair, 1966, walnut and curly maple, vacuum-formed back and seat, solid legs, made at R.I.T., 30" h x 20"d x 16" w. Ebner recalls:

> The seat and back were vacuumed formed and veneered. I first did the dining chair, then the occasional chair, because that is a much more complicated process in molding.

Round Dining Table and four chairs. The walnut and curly maple veneered top was David Ebner's first use of veneer, 1967.

Ebner's first, hand-carved bowl, birch, c. 1967, 19″ w x 9″ d x 4″ h. Ebner remembers:
   This was the first lessons in carving; Wendel (Castle) taught that. It included the use of gouges, mallets and scraper blades in the process of getting a form from a solid piece of wood using carving tools. It was an all-encompassing exercise in the carving procedure; quite valuable. What I learned on that piece I used for the rest of my working life.

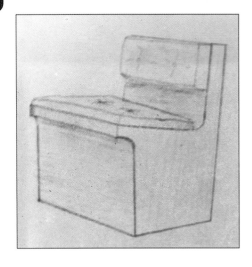

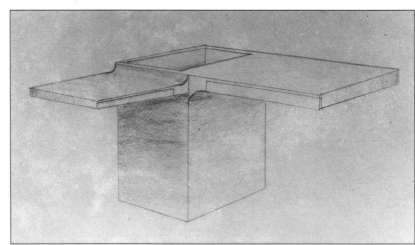

Ebner's B.F.A. Thesis Exhibit furniture was made at The Rochester Institute of Technology, in 1968. Drawings are of a matching chair and desk, the *Receptionist's Desk*, walnut, 30″ d x 40″ l x 38″ w, and the *Coffee Table* of rosewood and paint, 17″ h x 40″ w x 20″ d.

David Ebner graduated from the Rochester Institute of Technology in 1968, with a bachelor's degree in Fine Arts. He then took advanced study at the London School of Furniture Design and Production in England.

After returning home in 1969, he was drafted into the U.S. Army and assigned to a special exhibit unit in Washington, D.C. There he met two men from Long Island, painter Joe Riboli and boat-builder Jimmy Federenchick, who became life-long friends. When they left the Army in 1971, David traveled around the United States for a year and a half, before settling in a studio in Federenchick's garage at Bell Point, Long Island, New York.

Side Table and *Coffee Table*, c. 1969. Ebner says:
> A much later piece. It was done when I was in the military. It was salvaged material with finger-jointed construction, with a Formica top. Part of a series of tables I did when I was in the Army, in 1969-70.

Oak Liquor Cabinet, 1966, 37" h x 28" w x 18" d.

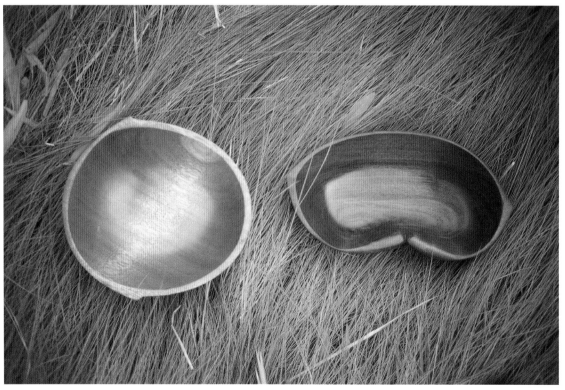

Sculptured wood, *Vessels,* c. 1968-1975. These hand-carved vessels were made after graduating from R.I.T. and before setting up his first studio at Blue Point, New York. The wooden vessels were first made at R.I.T., as exercises to begin learning to carve and use tools. Later, they were made as wedding presents to his friends. Thirty years on, some were cast in bronze. Ebner recalls:

A pair of carved bowls, using techniques I had learned at R.I.T. I did these because I was just out of the Army, I was taking a cross country year off, and to keep busy I brought gouges and a couple of clamps and a couple of blocks of wood. Wherever I stopped, I could do some carving. One is mahogany and one is teak. The rounder one is mahogany and the other one is teak. I actually did these before I set up my first studio.

Turned vessel of birds-eye maple with a little spalt in it, 6″ h x 12″ d.

Turned vessel in spalted maple, 12″ d x 3/16″ w x 6″ h.

Turned wooden vessel, 7" h x 10" d.

Turned vessel of ant-infested, spalted maple, 7" h x 12" d.

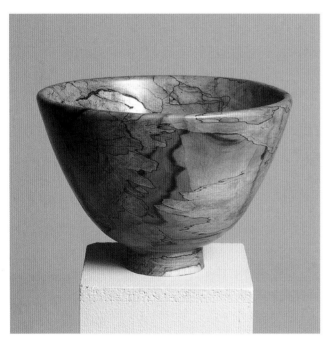

Turned vessel of spalted maple, 8" h x 10" d.

Turned vase of English brown oak burl, 11" h x 4.5" d.

1945—1972

Hollow-turned bowl of ant-infested red maple, 8" d x 7" h.

Turned bowl of wild cherry burl with a "wild edge," 6.5" h x 7" d.

Turned bowl of red oak burl with the bark left on, producing a "wild edge,d." 4" h x 6.5" d.

Turned bowl of red oak burl with a "wild edge," 5" h x 6.5" d.

His early interest in Frank Lloyd Wright led to his first exposure to Eastern art and design. In the early 1970s, reports Binzen,

> Ebner came across several books that deepened his interest in Asia. One was on Asian shrines, another was on calligraphy, and a third was on bamboo. He built a small table in cocobolo inspired by the shrines and designed a benchmark based on the calligraphy.
>
> Binzen, Op.cit.

Ebner's formal education and the early part of his career came on the heels of a nascent studio furniture movement. A document in the Pritam & Eames Gallery Archives describes creativity of the period:

> That furniture could have a personality as individual as its maker has been a trademark of the studio furniture movement ever since the first group of self-taught practitioners began their work in the early-to-mid 20th-century. Of these makers, Wharton Esherick, George Nakashima, Art Carpenter, Sam Maloof, and James Krenov are perhaps the best known of the era. They built one-of-a-kind, functional, mostly wood furniture. The codification of this approach—furniture as a means of self-expression—took place largely in the 1960s when the university became the standard training ground for craftsmen.
>
> It should come as no surprise that the cross-fertilization of ideas that a university environment fosters would inevitably give substance to the revolution brewing within traditional crafts. Craft mediums like glass, clay, and fiber seemed to absorb the functional and non-functional duality of their nature easily. However, because of its historical ties to use, furniture was probably the last of the craft disciplines to embrace the non-functional compact with contemporary art.

Ebner development reflects the changing milieu. As Rosenberg reports:

> David Ebner recalls having to make a conscious effort to give his pieces pleasing designs that also function well. When he began furniture-making at college, he was more concerned with the technique of making the pieces, and how it would suit its purpose when finished, and how it looked. His teacher advised him to look more closely at shapes around him and to try to use them to add more interest to his work. As an aid to observation, he developed the habit of sketching everyday objects that appealed to him. Twenty years later, Ebner rarely walks down a street or eats a meal without observing the forms. Each time he leaves his house, he stuffs his back pocket with four or five drawing pens. When he returns, he usually has several sketches made on napkins or scraps of paper, which he pins up on his shop wall. Eventually, a shape sketched at an idle moment will turn up in one of his pieces.
>
> Rosenberg, Op.cit., page 29

The David N. Ebner logo reflects the Eastern influence in his work.

Chapter 2
BLUE POINT STUDIO
1973–1975

Ink sketch portrait of David Ebner by
Charlotte Roe, late 1970s to early 1980s.

David Ebner lived at Blue Point, on Eastern Long Island, New York, from 1973 to 1975. His friend, Jimmy Federenchick, who he had met during their military service, also lived there. As Ebner told Barbara Delatiner in 1992:

> I remembered seeing all the Abstract Expressionists in the Albright-Knox Gallery in Buffalo, and the East End of Long Island looked like a great place to live. It was a place with an educated, sophisticated, and wealthy population that could afford and would appreciate what I wanted to do.
>
> I rented a room from Jimmy Federenchick and used his garage as my studio. I was off and running. Jimmy was the first of a few very helpful individuals to give me "a leg up," without which I would not have been able to get where I am today.
>
> "A Creator of 'Antiques of Tomorrow.'"
> *The New York Times*, Long Island
> edition, July 5, 1992, page 10

The yard in front of Ebner's first studio in Blue Point, New York, 1974. Photo by William Apton.

Jim Federenchick at the garage where Ebner had his first studio, in Blue Point, New York, 1973.

RENWICK STOOL

The design for a stool was made in 1974 with plank sides and a curved seat. He made it with black walnut wood, dovetail joined, glued, hand carved, and oiled, 17" h x 16" w x 15" d. It was exhibited in 1975 at the "Craft Multiples" show at the Renwick Gallery of the Smithsonian Institution in Washington, D.C., which opened on July fourth.

Oscar Fitzgerald described the exhibition:

Several of the pieces were submitted by craftsmen who would later become leaders in the field. Objects included a music stand by Wendell Castle, a wall unit by John Cederquist, and a stool by David Ebner. Castle's music stand represents the early work of craftsmen who went on to reinvent himself numerous times over his career. Without the provenance, it would be impossible to know simply by looking that the wall unit was created by John Cedarquist. Soon after making the cabinet, Cedarquist moved from art-deco-inspired casework to his familiar *trompe-l'oeil* creations. Ebner's stool was a prototype for what soon emerged as his signature piece, one he produces in bronze as well as wood.

Studio Furniture of the Renwick Gallery
Smithsonian American Art Museum.
Washington, D.C.: Smithsonian
American Art Museum, page 15

Ebner's stool, catalog number 110, was singled out as outstanding and selected for acquisition by the museum for its permanent collection. It has since become known as *The Renwick Stool*.

Over subsequent years, this stool design has been made in many different woods and also has been cast in bronze. The beauty and function of Ebner's 1974 Renwick Stool are ably described by Kari M. Main:

David Ebner relies on the beauty of wood grain for the artistic impact of this tranquil piece, while using exposed joinery as decoration…the concave seat of the stool mirrors, as in pagoda profiles and austere padouk seats, while comfortably cradling the sitter. The result is a successful blending of art with function, beauty and comfort.

Please Be Seated, Contemporary Studio
Seating Furniture. New Haven: Yale
University Art Gallery, 1999

The Renwick Stool, Zebrawood, 1975, 17" h x 16" w x 15" d.
This dove-tailed joint stool was first exhibited at the Renwick Gallery of the National Collection of Fine Arts, Smithsonian Institution, in Washington, D. C., where it was chosen for inclusion into the permanent collection. The form was also made later in cast bronze.

1973–1975

Caned Dining Chair, 1974.
This was David Ebner's first
commissioned piece

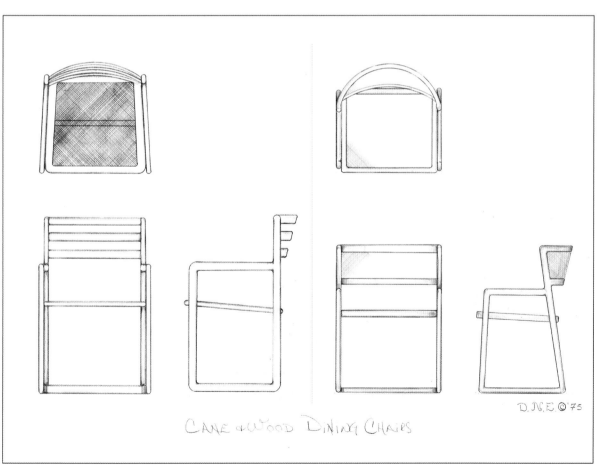

CANE & WOOD DINING CHAIRS

D.N.E. © '75

Drawings of the cane and wood dining chair, 1974.

Cherry stool, 1974, 17″ h x 15″ w x 14″ d.

1973–1975

Douglas fir chair, 1974, 32″ h x 22″ w x 22″ d.

Fir coffee table, 1974, 17" h x 40" w x 22" d.

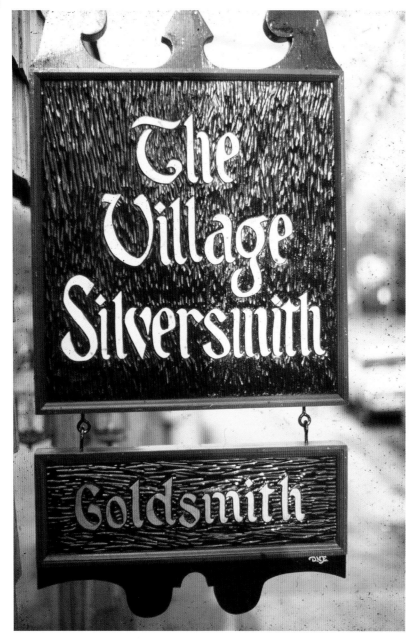

Carved shop sign of white cedar, 1974.

Carved house number sign and detail,
English brown oak, 1975.

Blanket Chest of white cedar wood, with a hinged lid incorporating a raised center and the front of the case with an oval inlay. This was one of Ebner's first studio pieces, 1973, 19" h x 40" w.x 22" d.

Rocking Horse, 1974, 19" d x 60" l x 40" h. This was an early studio piece made of carved Douglas fir and German yellow pine, made for Ebner's first major juried museum exhibition at the De Cordova Museum show in Lincoln, Massachusetts.

Another *Rocking Horse*, 1974, built from salvaged materials in darker Douglas fir wood, with a French enameling technique for the eyes and a sheepskin saddle cloth, hemp mane and tail, 19" d x 60" l x 40" h.

bed & board

"Bed and Board", the DeCordova Museum's third major Bicentenial exhibition, is devoted to contemporary quilts and woodwork. It's a bright, bold, innovative display, in striking contrast to the disciplined restraint of "Shaker Heritage". The contemporary works in "Bed and Board" and the early American pieces in "Shaker Heritage" testify to the profound changes which have taken place in American crafts over the past two centuries. The exhibition "Bed and Board" is funded in part by a grant from the National Endowment for the Arts.

From the exhibition "Bed and Board": "Rocking Horse", 1974, made from Douglas fir and German yellow pine, by David N. Ebner of Blue Point, N.Y.

Ebner's rocking horse was first shown at the 1975 Exhibition "Bed and Board" and concerts held at the De Cordova Museum and Sculpture Park in Lincoln, Massachusetts.

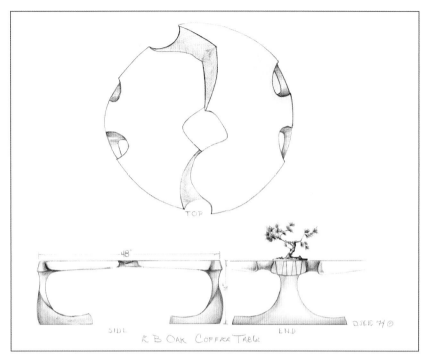

Drawing of a coffee table, English brown oak, 1975, 17" h. x 50" w. x 48" d.

Glass-topped *Coffee table*, 1975.

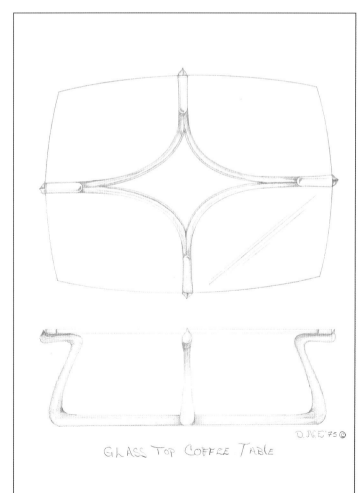

Wall Shelf with a shaped shelf, 1975.

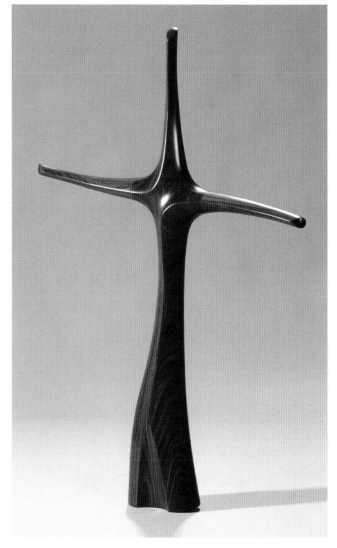

Cross of carved tulip wood, commissioned as a dance figure, 1975, 44″ h x 24″ w x 4″ d. Ebner remembers:
    The cross was a commission for a non-denominational church in Sayville, New York, one of the few rhetorical pieces that I've worked on. I was really trying to get the idea of dance and celebration into the crucifix; more of celebration of life than of death. That piece is in tulip wood. Probably the first one was done in the wormy chestnut in the Blue Point studio and I remade that piece three or four times over about a ten-year period.

Rectangular zebrawood
Sofa Table, the first of
this form, made in 1975.
Courtesy of Moderne Gallery

Ladderback side chair of bird's eye maple, 1974, 34" h x 16" w x 16" d.

The second studio of David
Ebner was in a red-painted hay
barn, in Brookhaven Hamlet,
New York.

Chapter 3
BROOKHAVEN HAMLET STUDIO
1976–1984

In 1976, Ebner moved farther east and settled in
Brookhaven Hamlet, Long Island, New York, where he
also enjoyed the golf and fishing facilities. It took a period
of adjustment, Ebner recalled:

> I realized that I wanted the entire hands-on
> experience...from concept to final product and even sales.
> Most people are delegated to one aspect. I wanted it all.
>
> Delatiner, Op.cit.

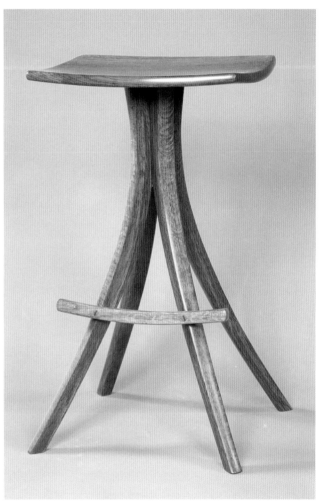

Stool #1 of red oak, 1976, made in various heights from low to
counter-height, using tapered laminates in a re-sawn technique
and a carved seat on four splayed legs with a stretcher-footrest.
This was the first design of the later bamboo stools with a metal
stretcher.

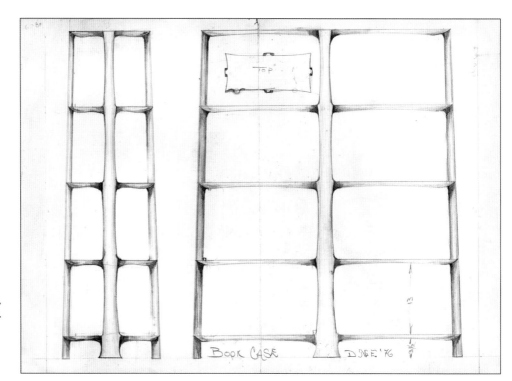

Drawing for a bookcase, 1976.

1976–1984

Oak End Table, 1977,
20″ h x 18″ w x 26″ d

STERNUM DESIGNS

Ebner's attention to and use of the world around him in his designs is evident in his "Sternum Bone Series," a music stand, tables, a rocking chair, and other forms that had their origins in a duck bone.

This was the series of using the sternum bone of a duck as the inspiration for the designs. That bone came off my dinner table after having duck. The sternum bone is really a structural bone, not like a wish bone, because a chickens don't really fly that much. The sternum bone connects the muscles to the wings in birds of flight. That's why I call it the sternum bone series. It also showed me cantilever. I put the bone down, it started rocking. Back then, everyone felt they had to do a rocking chair, a music stand.

I had done a couple corner tables, music stand, dictionary stand, and a glass top table using that bone as the inspiration for that series of pieces. A lot of times throughout the period of making this body of work, I would pick a design or a design inspiration, and do something like sculptors would do; I would do a study, I would use it in a number of different ways, and after I felt I exhausted the study, then I would move on. The corner tables were the first of the bone pieces, the rocking chair was a part of that series, and the last was what I call the *Bone Coffee Table*, the zebra wood table with the glass top. So there was a whole series of pieces.

I've explored a variety of directions and themes over the years, but each piece is treated as an art object, with concern for my material and honesty to its inherent qualities.

David Ebner has no problem combining traditional and modern techniques. That is, he will use hand-cut dovetails as joints, as well as contemporary adhesives and metal fasteners. Again, Ebner admits:

There's nothing wrong with growth through progress… and structurally, I want to make sure that two hundred years form now all my work will remain sound.

Delatiner, Op.cit.

The duck sternum bone that inspired many early pieces, including music and book stands, rocking chairs, and coffee tables. Ebner comments:

I approach my art intuitively as well as intellectually, drawing inspiration wherever I find it. I've explored a variety of directions and themes over the years, but each piece is treated as an art object with concern for my material and honesty to its inherent qualities. For me, one's creative ability is demonstrated in the diversity of the pieces and what one learns from change.

Worcester Center for Crafts, "The Chair" exhibit catalog, 2002, page 22

1976–1984

STERNUM DESIGNS

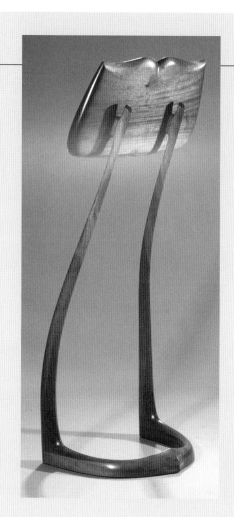

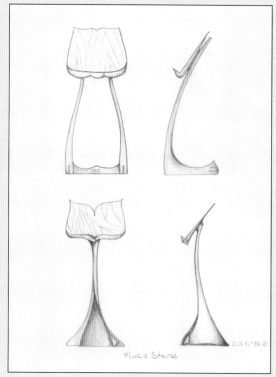

Music Stand of mahogany. This was one of David Ebner's first commissions, 1975, 54" h x 6" w x 20" d.

Sternum Dictionary or *Book Stand*, made with brown English oak, 1975, 22" w x 17" d x 40" h.

Square Coffee Table, with a two-part curving base, padouk, 1976, 17" h x 34"w x 34" d. The shape was inspired by a sternum bone from a duck. This was Ebner's first use of the sternum-bone design in furniture.

Ebner making a sternum rocking chair, 1976.

1976–1984

STERNUM DESIGNS

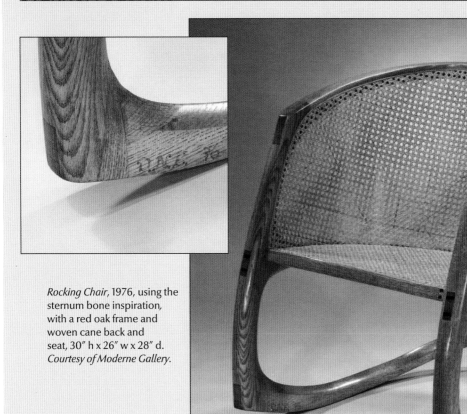

Rocking Chair, 1976, using the sternum bone inspiration, with a red oak frame and woven cane back and seat, 30" h x 26" w x 28" d. *Courtesy of Moderne Gallery.*

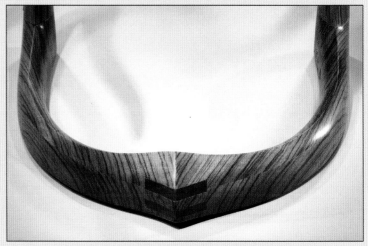

Sternum base details in zebra wood. Courtesy of Moderne Gallery.

Ebner and his pet cat, Thor, with a sternum coffee table, one of his early sternum pieces, 1978.

Sternum-bone Coffee Table, 1978, zebrawood and glass, 17" h x 38" w x 52" d.

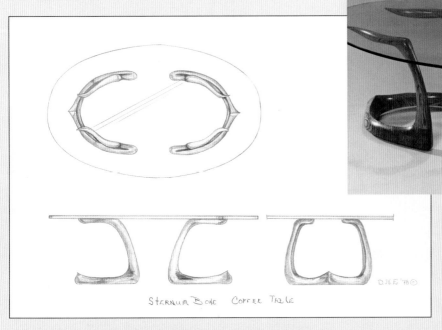

STERNUM BONE COFFEE TABLE

Sternum Coffee Table, 1978 to 1980s.

The organic, natural form of the Sternum Bone Series is not atypical of Ebner. In a 1979 critique, Helen A. Harrison wrote:

> David Ebner avoids the geometric in his furniture, preferring sensuous form with curves and bulges that emphasize the natural contours of the wood and take advantage of its organic quality. Mr. Ebner seems frequently to refer to Scandinavian design precedents, although his maple blanket chest suggests the influence of Art Nouveau.

She was not entirely smitten, however:

> It would be gratifying to see this gifted and accomplished craftsman working in a less derivative plastic vocabulary.
>
> "Objects that combine Practicality with Beauty," *The New York Times*, Long Island edition, page 17, July 1, 1979.)

Coffee table with a square mahogany base, chiseled texture, and a round glass top, 38" d x 16" h.

Bookcase of mahogany, c. 1978, 84" h x 108" w x 16"d.

David N. Ebner's initials and the year of construction, 1977, on a mahogany, open storage case for LP records.

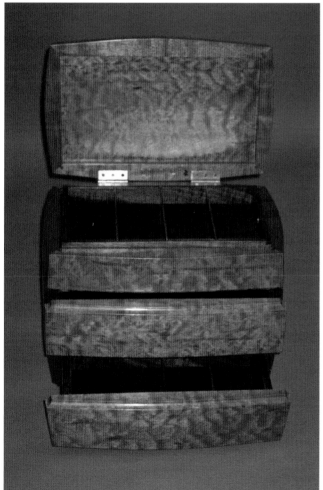

Three-drawer *Jewelry Box,* of quilted mahogany with a carved and hinged top, 1978, 16″ w x 12″ h x 10″ d.

Jewelry Box of wormy chestnut, 16″ w x 12″ h x 10″ d.

Mirror of lacewood, c. 1980s, 64" l x 42" w.

Coffee Table, an early studio design in David Ebner's "Classic Impressions" series, purpleheart, 1978. 17" h x 52" w x 20" d.

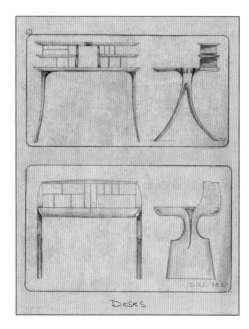

Drawing of *Desks*, 1978.

1976–1984

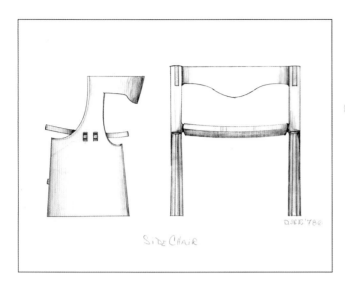

Drawing of *Side Chair,* 1978.

Wall Sculpture, maple, in rectangular shape with protruding sections, late 1970s, 32" h x 60" w x 15" d.

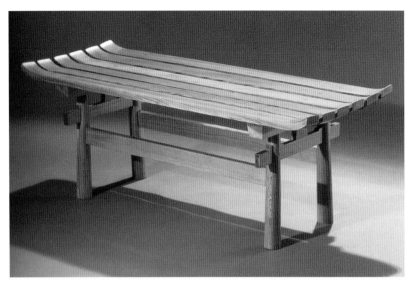

This *Bench,* late 1970s, was inspired by a Japanese Tori gate. It has a Douglas fir slatted top, with up-turned ends and four flaring legs joined by plank stretchers. 15" h x 60"w x 15"d.

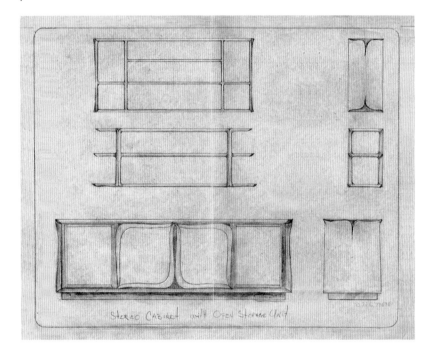

STEREO CABINET with OPEN STORAGE UNIT

Stereo Cabinet, 1979, English brown oak and ash burl doors.

Unique *Low Stool* of laminated mahogany, with a seat modeled after a tractor seat and columnar base. The piece was commissioned by a grower of Cala lilies, 1979.

A two-piece *Coffee Table*, 1979, in wormy chestnut wood, 17″ h x 42″ w x 22″ d.

Dining Table of English brown oak with an octagonal top and panel-sided, pedestal base, 1979, 54" d x 30" h.

A view of the base during finishing.

Console Table, 1979, with a rectangular top dovetailed to the supports. The form also has been made as a desk, with a shelf and a top.

Blanket Chest, sapele with hand-forged, bronze handles, late 1970s to 2008. 22" h x 36"w x 22"d. Soft, rounded, bulbous forms take the tension out of the straight planes. The design for this evolved over several years, with refinements. A drawer in the bottom was incorporated because of Ebner's knowledge of clever, Shaker utilization of all the space in a form.

1976–1984

A double-pedestal variation of the *Dining Table*, 1979.

Redwood *Settee,* 1979, 30" h x 42" w x 20" d.

Purpleheart *Coatrack,* on a marble base.

SCALLIONS/ONIONS

David Ebner's early scallions/onions designs were predicated in a small book, *Chives, Their Wit and Wisdom*, by Rose Quong, Cobble Hill Press, New York, 1968. The images in the book inspired Ebner and forecast his onions/scallions pieces.

His first "onion" design appears in a sketch book from his Brookhaven Hamlet, red barn studio. Ebner recalls:

These came about because I was sketching at lunch one day, and that red barn was next to a leased farmer's field, and they were growing onions.

The onion chest is one of my favorite stacked pieces I've done, I like the scale of it. I think what makes both that and the scallion coat rack so successful, people are amused when they see something out of scale. I brought it into human scale, I want you to walk up to it as it was human scale. That is probably my most reproduced pieces, the *Scallion Coat Rack*. Only because it became, once I learned how to make the piece, a lathe project; that made it a lot easier to make. Also, I like the idea that you don't know if I made it yesterday or thirty years ago. I thought about it as a student early on, you want to make things that people walk up to and say, "What period did this come out of?" Then you know you have really achieved this captured moment, a timeless moment.

The chest was two months in construction and made with stacked lamination, a technique learned at R.I.T. with Wendell Castle. David Ebner stayed away from using this Castle-based technique for many years, until he could make it in his own style.

Now it is an edition that is still alive, and was made in bronze, where the design becomes pure sculpture. The patina is an important feature of the bronze form.

David Ebner acknowledges the contributions of his co-workers in his studio:

I want to acknowledge that no one person does this big a body of work. I've always had help throughout all the years. I've watched the help have input in to how we make the things. On this piece here [*Monumental Scallion*], my helper at the time, who is still working with me for over 35 years, now part time, was Alfred Roe. His father was somewhat of an inventor. His great-grandfather held the patent of the first tape measure and held a number of patents, including the first crank for an awning mechanism. His father had said it would be a lot easier if you put it [the big scallion] on the lathe. I said, "What are you talking about?" I found I could just make a very simple jig and fixture. That's what you see in these photographs. It is how I was able to mount and hold this without it wobbling all over. It was called a "steady rest." It was my helper's father's influence that turned one or two pieces of an item; I've now made 130 or 140, which is nice.

I think it was very important, when I was working on a piece and I really liked what I was doing, I would make extra parts and that enabled me to [enter a] show. A lot of people would have to stop. It's so not cost effective to stop for six months or a year. If they thought about making an extra one, or making the parts for an extra one and putting it aside, first finish your commission work, or whatever, and then you have enough pieces to put together for a show. If the public doesn't see the work, you can be good—but you have to get it in the public's eye. I always wanted to get the work out, [have it be] seen as much as possible; that's where multiple pieces work out and you can show that way; you can afford to show that way.

Onion Chest, red oak, bleached and painted ash, 1979, 30" d x 44" h; also 28" d x 54" h.

SCALLIONS/ONIONS

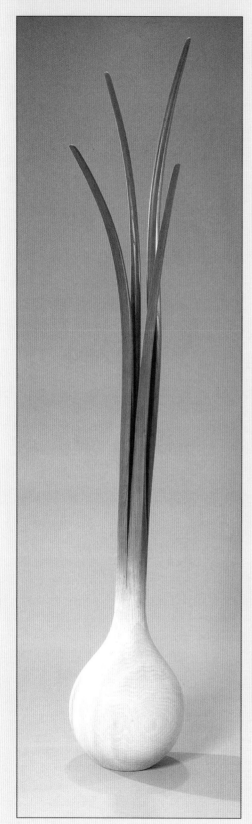

A *Monumental Scallion* under construction.

Scallion Coat Rack, 1983, stacked and laminated northern white ash, bleached and painted, 69" h x 19" w x 12" d. The onion became a *Scallion Coat Rack* and was popular because of its size. Ebner wanted to make it a functional sculpture.

TWISTED STICKS

Willie Smith, who successfully designed "Willywear" in New York City was a friend of Ebner's. He exposed Ebner to African tribal arts and advocated not doing too much to natural materials.

In a similar vein, a 1972 exhibit of furniture by Wharton Esherick (1887–1970)—the Pennsylvania, pioneer studio furniture artist who preferred Pennsylvania wood—impressed Ebner. Esherick incorporated natural forms and materials into his work with minimal manipulation. He once said that "If I can't make something beautiful out of what I find in my backyard, I had better not make anything."

Twisted sassafras and maple sticks choked by honeysuckle grew plentifully in the area of Ebner's Long Island studio. He decided to make something beautiful out of these readily available materials. He recalls:

> I took a look at what was around and noticed all these honeysuckle vines that grow around the wood. So I stripped the bark off and gave it a bone look by sanding it.
>
> Cromeyn, Op.cit.

His "Twisted Sticks" series developed from that thinking. The first stick piece, a glass-topped coffee table, was followed by the *Book Chair*. Ebner comments:

> Man's first furniture was likely made from the sicks and bones he found in his immediate surroundings. Likewise, the twisted sticks and spalted wood I use are found, native materials. The majority are sassafras, a fast-growing, under-utilized native species, seldom employed for furniture.
>
> My twisted-stick furniture puts no demand on the forest or lumber industries. These native spalted woods have all the richness and excitement of tropical woods, but are discarded natural materials at the end of their life-cycles, which, if not used, would simply rot entirely.
>
> *Conservation by Design*. Providence: Museum of Art, Rhode island School of Design, 1993, page 90

These twisted sassafras sticks are right out of the woods.

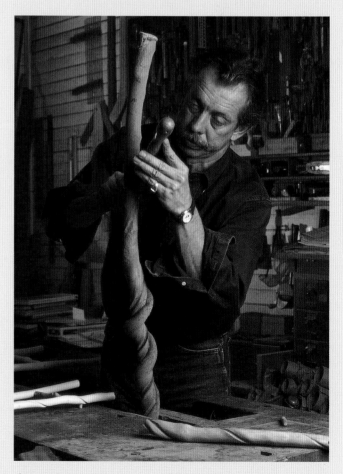

Ebner making an early, twisted-stick furniture form, 1979.

Twisted-sticks Dining Table, the first stick piece Ebner made, sassafras and glass, 1979, 30" h x 84" l x 36" w.

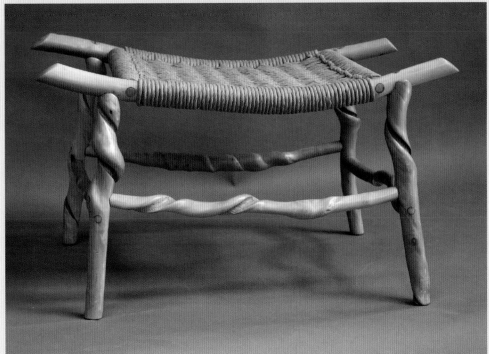

Twisted-sticks footstool. 13" h x 24" w x 15" d.

TWISTED STICKS

These three, wall-mounted ladders of twisted sticks were inspired by a visit to Mesa Verde, New Mexico, where kiva ladders are seen in perspective. Here they appear as sculpture in an exhibition of David Ebner's work.

Three wall-mounted ladders of twisted sticks, ca. 1979.

A *Twisted-sticks Ladder-back Side Chair* is formed with sassafras and a woven rush seat, 1993, 80" h x 20" w x 18" d.

The *Twisted-sticks Foyer Table*
with sassafras frame and legs,
rosewood top, 1995, 25" h x 60" w x 15" d.

A *Twisted-sticks Three-panel Screen* frame of sassafras supports and silk that was woven and embroidered with trees and a river scene by Pamela Toppin, 1996, 25" h x 36" w.

TWISTED STICKS

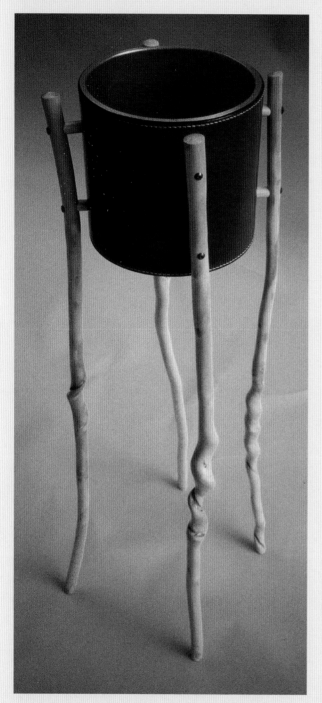

The *Twisted-sticks Plant/Wine Bucket Stand* with a copper liner supported by twisted sassafras sticks, 1997, 36" h x 10" d.

The *Twisted-sticks Coffee Table* with legs pierced through the glass top, 199 17" h x 32" w x 17" d.

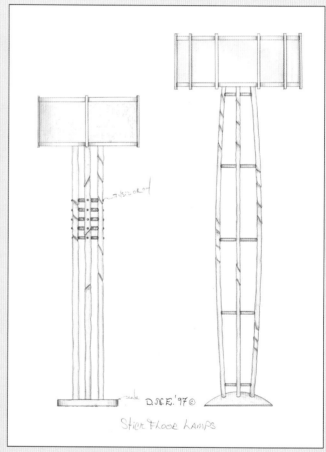

The drawing for the *Twisted-sticks Floor Lamps*, 1997.

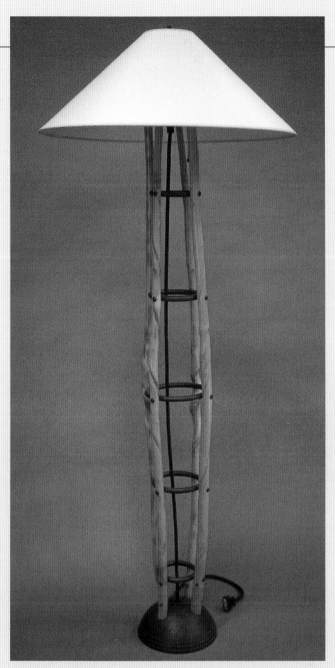

Book Chair, 1998, made with local twisted sassafras wood supports and spalted maple seat, 24" h x 17" w x 15" d.

Twisted-sticks Floor Lamp, 1997, 55" h x 8" w x 8" d.

Twisted-sticks chair of sassafras and spalted maple, with a grahite-darkened lacquer finish, 2007, 20" w x 16" d x 25" h.

TWISTED STICKS

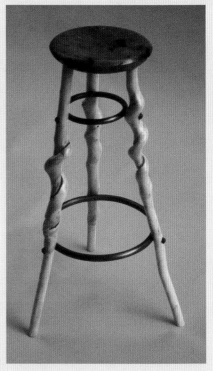

Twisted-sticks Bench variation, of sassafras with a woven seat, 15" h x 36" w x 15" d.

A *Twisted-sticks Counter Stool* of sassafras, cherry burl seat and metal, 2000, 25" h x 13" w x 8" d.

Ebner has made chairs and tables that evoke the grace of extended branches, sometimes using wood that has been twisted and choked by honeysuckle. His *Scallion Hat Rack* and *Twisted Stick Candlesticks* satisfy as both sculpture and functional art. As Cromeyn has noted, "His 'twisted wood' style is a classic mark of his work, which he has used to make everything from chairs to footstools and even menorah candle holders."

Twisted-sticks Menorahs with twisted sassafras stick bases, 2000, 12" h x 20" w x 4" d.

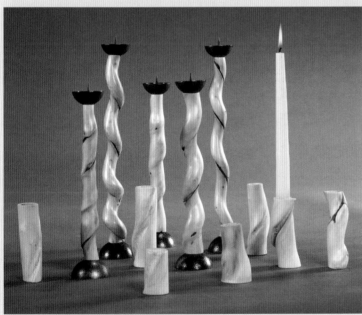

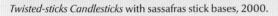

Twisted-sticks Candlesticks with sassafras stick bases, 2000.

TWISTED STICKS

Twisted-sticks Table Lamp, maple, alabaster shade, with hand-peaned and blued metal, 2001, 17″ h x 10″ d.

Fireplace Tool Set made with twisted sassafras sticks. The handles and base support are forged metal with brass, 2001, 32″ h x 12″ d.

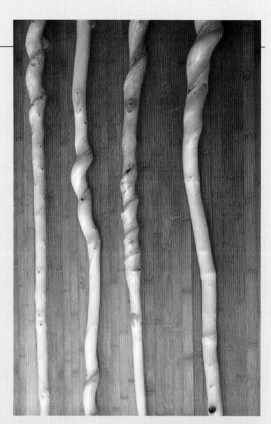

Detail of the library shelves' end wall.

The ends of these bookshelves are enhanced with twisted sticks on a bamboo background, at the library in Bellport, New York, 2002.

TWISTED STICKS

Twisted-sticks Stool made from sassafras, 2006, 15" h x 16" w x 14" d.

Twisted-sticks bench made with sassafras and rush seats, 2006, 16" h x 48" w x 15" d.

A unique form was created in sassafras when two *Twisted-stick Foot Stools* were joined to form a bench. David recalls it was fun to make, and the design was successful. The form was inspired by the tool handles he had used in collaboration with Ivan Barnett, 1995, 60" w x 15" d x 15" h.

Twisted-sticks Side or *Desk Chair* supported with thirteen twisted sassafras sticks, white oak back, and leather seat, 2008, 21" w x 22" d x 30" h.

Detail of the seat construction.

Twisted-sticks Serving Table with curly cherry top, 28" h x 60" w x 16" d.

TWISTED STICKS

Twisted-sticks Hall Table with chestnut top, 32" h x 40" w x 20" d.

Merging Inclinations Bench, pigmented sassafras, lacewood, and slate. This was a later "Twisted-sticks" piece with a graphite-darkened finish to take out the grain in this sassafras frame, 16.5" h x 69" w x 15.5" d.

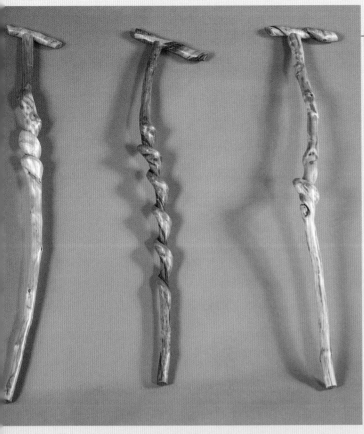

Box ornamented with a twisted stick, 6.5″ h x 10″ w x 6″ d.

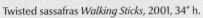

Twisted sassafras *Walking Sticks*, 2001, 34″ h.

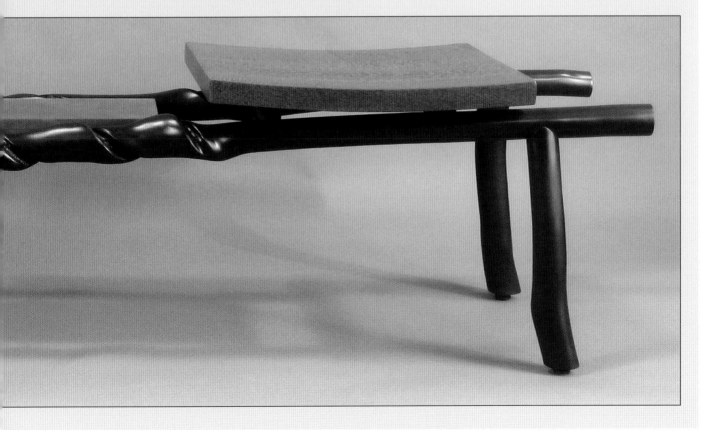

One-legged *Corner Table*, early 1980s.
This table was inspired by European
Art Nouveau furniture and re-designed
for the "Classic Impressions" series.

Wall Box with steam-bent afromosia wood and a calf-skin-
covered door, 1981, 15" w 8" d x 4" h.

Corner Table of mottled mahogany with an
oil finish, early 1980s, 26" w x 18" d x 30" h.

This unique pair of three-shelf *Book Cart* units was made in English brown oak, 1981, 32″ w x 14″ d x 36″ h.

Wall-mounted *Tool Box* made of mahogany, 1982, 36″ w x 10″ d x 35″ h.

Gate-leg Table of curly maple with an oil finish, first made in 1981, 46″ d x 30″ h.

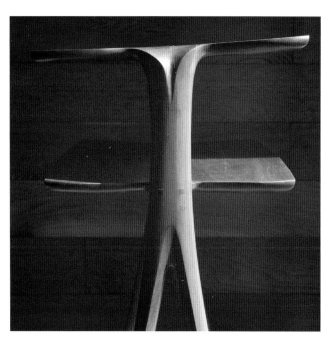

Book Stand or *Standing Desk*, an early design first made in 1978, cherry, 1982, 32″ w x 19″ d x 39″ h.

Desk, walnut with leather top, 1982.

The *Writing Chair*, also known as the *Brookhaven Chair*, is one of Ebner's signature pieces. An extension of his *Sofa Table* in re-sawn laminates and made to accompany a desk, it has been called "comfortable, unique, and structurally sound." He carries the theme forward in the design for the *Library Steps*.

Writing Chair, 1983, one shown in red oak and one in zebrawood, 20" w x 20" d x 28.25" h.

Tripod Wine Table, 1984, 24" h x 18" d.

Dressing/Foyer Mirror with a pagoda-shaped top, shown in purpleheart, 1984, 44" w x 3" d x 82" h.

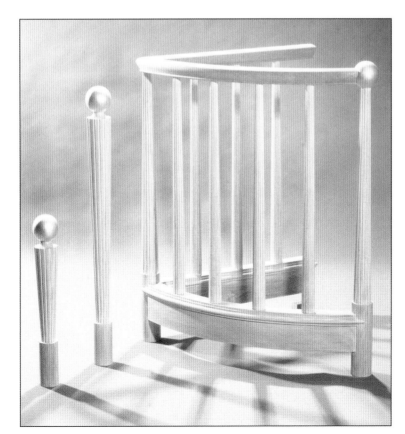

Details of a *Spiral Staircase*, bleached white with white silver leaf, 1984.

Back view

Interior view

Liquor Cabinet, walnut, 1984, 32″ w x 20″ d x 54″ h. David Ebner comments:
This walnut liquor cabinet, with hand-cut dovetails for the carcass, has a solid, floating panel in the front doors and the material that was left after I cut the panels for the front doors was put together in a collage panel for the back. I felt this was much more becoming than the front doors, much more effective. The design for the piece was inspired by how Wharton Esherick put wall paneling on the floor in his kitchen in his house; he used natural form boards that were spliced together, which I intend to revisit again.

Game Table with reversible leather top and ebonized oak skirt and legs, 1984, 28″ w x 28″ d x 30″ h.

Corner Table, maple, 1984, 22″ w x 22 d x 30″ h.

Writing Desk and *Chair,* English brown oak and burl top, c. 1984.

Coffee Table, mahogany, with an oval top, 1981, 50" w x 32" d x 17" h.

Coffee Table, with a long cocobolo plank top, early 1980s.

Museum of Fine Arts (MFA) Bench, 1984, purpleheart. Also made in painted wood, 15" h x 16" d x 38" w. The bench was later cast in bronze, in 2002, in an edition of fifteen, 17" h x 15.5" d x 36" w.

CHAPTER 4
BELLPORT STUDIO
1985–2004

David Ebner conversing
in his home, 2000.

The third studio of David Ebner was at 12 Bell Street, Bellport, New York, in a building that was formerly a hardware store. It is now owned by the Brookhaven Historical Society. Ebner did a major renovation to the building during his tenure, from 1985 to 2004.

In an 1986 interview with Betty Kartalis for *Shore Lines* magazine, Ebner reflected on the continual demands of designing furniture:

> It is a challenge...to make the product visually pleasing and still have it function.
>
> "Breaking the Barrier between
> Craftsman and Artist," *Shore Lines*,
> June, 1986

The Bellport Studio before and after renovation.

Far left:
Two-drawer Filing Cabinet, sapele wood, 1985, 17″ w x 23″ d x 27″ h.

Left:
Sofa Table, first made in 1975, this table was made with afromosia wood in 1985, 58″ w x 14″ d x 25″ h.

Cabinet, Desk and *Chair*, English brown oak, 1985. Desk 48″ w x 29″ d x 30″ h. Chair 20″ w x 20″ d x 30″ h.

Lingerie Chest of Drawers, mahogany, 1985, 24" w x 14" d x 44" h. The design was inspired by Ebner's 1965 *Chest of Drawers*.

CHEST OF DRAWERS

LINGERIE Chest

Low Boy

D.N.E. 2005©

Drawing for David Ebner's *Chest of Drawers, Lingerie Chest*, and *Low Boy*.

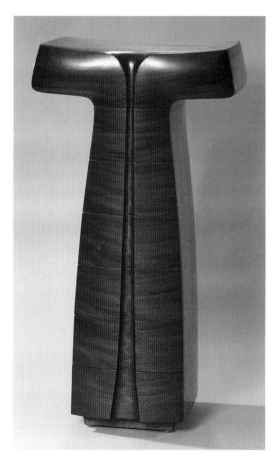

Lingerie Chest, made in a different wood, in 1985.

Suite of Suede-upholstered Seating made on commission, 1986. Swivel barrel chair with wenge wood detail, 30″ w x 28″ d x 30″ h.

Loveseat in Belgian wool
and purpleheart arms and
base, 1989.

"The Room," an exhibit of Ebner's
work, July 3 to August 5, 1986, at
the Pritam & Eames Gallery

Fireplace Surround made with
fluted uprights and a mantle
shelf, 1986. This view was part
of "The Room" show in 1986.

1985–2004

A square *Side Table* with a purpleheart frame, ebony detail and a molded edge, resting on four straight tapering legs, 1986, 12″ l x 12″ w x 22″ h.

Another square *Side Table* in mahogany with rosewood detail and a book-matched, crotch mahogany, veneered top, resting on four straight tapering legs, 1987, 12″ l x 12″ we x 22″ h.

Drawing of a ceiling-hung, wooden *Candelabra*, 1987.

One of two *Chandeliers* made by David Ebner in 1987, to accompany a dining table made by Sam Maloof. They hung from the ceiling for candles.

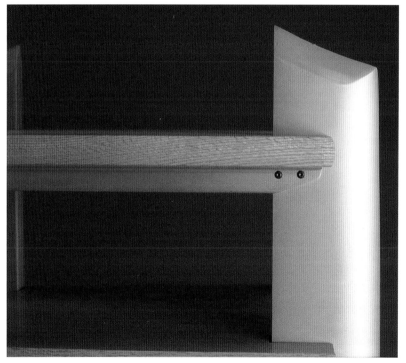

Pouvé-inspired *Storage Unit,* made as a commission in 1988, cast aluminum and oak. Six rectangular oak shelves are supported by cast-aluminum uprights, 16" d x 30" w x 60" h.

TUBULAR METAL, 1986

The designs for Ebner's tubular metal furniture, begun in 1986, were inspired by Marcel Breuer's Bauhaus-era style of around 1925. Ebner has made the style in coffee tables, end tables, desks, a desk chair, and a rocking chair. He employed a technician who could weld very carefully to make them fluid.

Two *Side Tables* of tubular metal and glass tops, 1992, 12" d x 22" h.

Three-tier Coffee Table, 1986, tubular metal with a custom, gunmetal finish, 18" h x 20" d x 40" l.

The *Sternum Rocking Chair* form also was made later with a tubular steel frame, mid-1980s.

Tubular metal desk chair on wheels, with black or gunmetal finish, mid-1980s, 24" w x 24" d x 32" h.

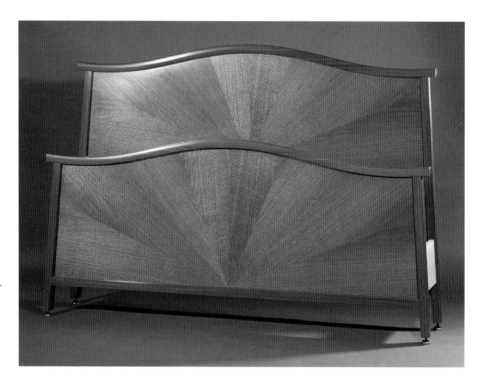

A *Sofa Table* with a rectangular top and two pedestal legs with splayed feet, made in several wood types including bleached, rift, white oak, 1988. Ebner comments:

This is one of the pieces where I have put some dramatic changes over the years, until I became happy with the way it flowed. I haven't changed it since I added the pour and the tear-drop shape to the leg.

Bed, 1989, lacewood, queen size.

Bed, 1989, quartered white oak, king size.

In a review of the six-artist invitational show entitled "In the Craft Tradition" at the Guild Hall Museum, Robert Long described David Ebner's work as:

> ...exquisitely crafted. [He] makes a variety of tables and chairs and other furnishings, which range from what he calls "classical impressions of furniture" to sculptural furniture and sculpture.
>
> "Exquisite Artistry of Crafts in Guild Hall Exhibition," *Southampton Press*, December 21, 1989.

Ebner amplified what he meant by "classical impressions:"

> ...the interpretation of traditional furniture forms in a contemporary way. I do this by removing embellishments and by using classical proportions.
>
> Ibid.

Ebner exhibited ten pieces in the 1989 Guild Hall Museum exhibition. Robert Long gave a concise, complimentary description of each peice:

> His "Rocker," in red oak, and "Music Stand" in Brazilian mahogany, are graceful, organically suggestive forms which bring Hector Guimard and the stylized contours of Art Moderne to mind.
>
> "Demi-lune" and "Mirror" , a bevel-edged mirror in the shape of a slightly squashed octagon, and an accompanying two-legged table, which attaches to a wall, are crafted in purple heart, an unworldly wood the color of red cabbage.
>
> "Desk and Chair" are made of butterfly English oak; the table top is burled. The table has an extremely delicate, wafer-like quality; the chair's legs, which grow organically from the simple backrest, are splayed and suggest a walking figure.

Blanket Chest, 1990, curly maple with an over-hanging, hinged lid and curly maple base molding, 44" w x 22" d x 21" h.

A rosewood stool, whose paddle-like legs are as pure in form as a Brancusi sculpture, is installed next to a small ladder-back chair in warm birds-eye maple with a leather seat.

Mr. Ebner's "Onion [Scallion] Coat Rack" is a witty, 69-inch-tall onion [scallion] whose long green shoots act as coat hooks; the white onion bulb acts as base and anchor.

"Lingerie Chest", in Honduran mahogany, is a stunning piece in the shape of a softened "T" or a stylized human figure; its seven drawers are fit nearly flush to the edges of the chest and follow its contours.

An 82- by 44-inch "Mirror" framed in red oak, is surmounted by a Japanese detail like the roof of a pagoda. The mirror is edged with strips of silver leaf.

Ibid.

♦♦♦

Ten Arrow Gallery, in Cambridge, Massachusetts, held a show called "Lathe-turned Furniture" in early 1990, where writer Christine Temin saw Ebner's furniture.

"One of the most discreet and innocent works in the show is Ebner's curly maple gateleg table, which has no exotic woods, no tour-de-force techniques, no eye-catching outline. A quiet version of a worthy classic, it's one of the most satisfying pieces in this fine exhibition."
"Lathe Works Star In Furniture Show,"
Boston Globe, February 1, 1990.

Jewelry Box of mahogany and rosewood, with a hinged lid and interior compartments. It was designed and made by Al Roe, who has been a studio assistant to Ebner for forty years.

ENDANGERED SPECIES SERIES

Ebner's *Endangered Species* series, made in 1989, was inspired by his trip to Mesa Verde and the Hopi Indians' lands in 1972. There he witnessed the symbolic designs of sandpaintings and images of the Southwest Indian culture. He carried these images in his head for seventeen years and put them to use in these sculptural forms.

An example of the Endangered Species series was exhibited in the "International Lathe-turned Objects Challenge IV" at the Port of History Museum, in Philadelphia, Pennsylvania in 1991. In the catalog description, Ebner wrote:

> The *Endangered Species* series is a group of sculptures executed to depict my apprehension about the state and future of the natural environment. In this body of new work, metaphysical concerns take precedence over utilitarian ones. The process used in the creation of these works reflects nature's own way of sculpting. Sandblasting was employed to create surface texture and fire, because of its spiritual and metaphysical qualities. The forms resulting from these methods—like nature—have a spherical sense with no beginning and no end.
>
> Wood Turning Center, Inc.
> Catalog for *International Lathe-turned Objects Challenge IV*, 1991, page 67.

Declining Species, 1989, wall sculpture of spalted beech, cherry burl, and a bluefish jaw bone, 15" d x 4" h.

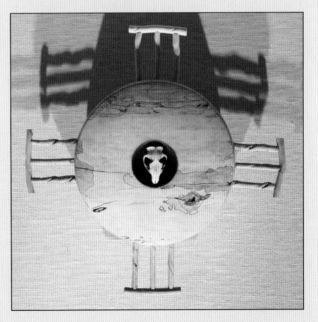

Spalted Prayers sculpture, 1989; carved maple, sassafras and bone, 27" d x 4" h.

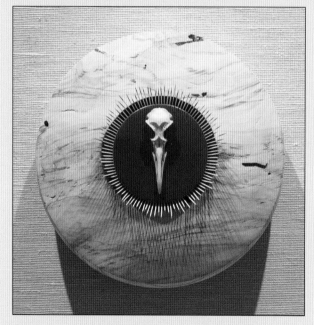

A portion of the *Endangered Species Series* in spalted beech, gull skull, and porcupine quills.

BELLPORT OUTDOOR SEATING

Bellport is a small, quiet town on the southern coast of Long Island, 65 miles from New York City. Ebner once described it as "chock-full of white houses surrounded by white picket fences and sprawling lawns." [Quoted in Jan Tyler, "The Bellport Bench," *The New York Times*, July 15, 1990]

The Bellport outdoor seating series represents Ebner's designs from the 1990s that were inspired by the picket fences in Bellport, and by the ocean waves and sand ripples. As contemporary furniture, they are executed in mahogany and spray-painted white.

> I used white to complement the image... The unpainted weathered effect just isn't right for Bellport... It's a way of aligning myself with a place of great charm, and an acknowledgment of the community where I live.
>
> John Perreault, Exhibiton Catalog, "Explorations II, The New Furniture," New York City: The American Craft Museum, 1991, page 15

The Bellport benches and chairs were first shown in the exhibit "Sitting Pretty," at Pritam & Eames Gallery, East Hampton, Long Island, New York, July 15–August 7, 1990. Helen A. Harrison, reviewing the exhibit for the *New York Times* wrote:

> Actually, a matching group of high-style outdoor furniture that includes a chair, chaise, tables, and benches, the Bellport suite was inspired by the look of the picturesque old village [Bellport, New York]. Designed to make an emphatic statement on green lawns, the furniture is painted white to reflect Ebner's perception of the Bellport charisma.
>
> "The Bellport Bench," *The New York Times*, July 15, 1990

Bellport Outdoor Bench, straight, 1990, 60" w x 18" d x 30" h.

Bellport Outdoor Bench, curved, 1990, 60" w x 18" d x 30" h.

BELLPORT OUTDOOR SEATING

Bellport Garden Chairs, 1990, mahogany, marine plywood, and teak, 33" x 29" x 24"

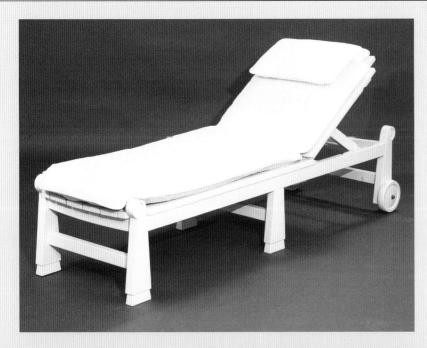

Bellport Lounge with adjustable back.

Ebner's renovated furniture-making studio, with the Bellport outdoor furniture collection shown in the storefront windows, 1990.

MORLEY CHAIRS

The *Morley Chair* is an updated version of the dining chair David Ebner made for the painter Malcolm Morley, who is a neighbor and friend of Ebner's.

As John Perreault has observed, commissions are "anathema" to most artists. He notes, however, that "Ebner welcomes them as a way of developing new forms." [Perreaut, Op.cit., p.16]

Ebner has described the Morley chair as a

> ...healthy, comfortable chair, fashioned from curly cherry and wenge. The chair was designed so that Mr. Morley and his guests could sit comfortably for hours at dinner.

In 1991, The American Craft Museum, in New York City, held an exhibit of new furniture designs, including works by Ebner. These chairs were exhibited there.

Morley Chair prototype (above) and finished examples.
33" h x 18" w x 19" d.

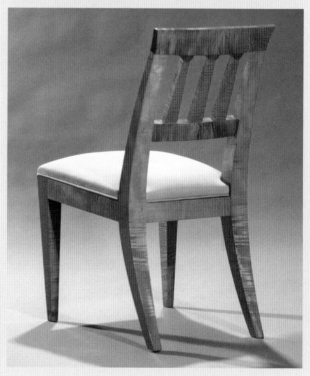

VALET RACK

In the Spring of 1992, David Ebner's mahogany and ebony *Valet Rack* was exhibited in the Early Spring Show at Pritam & Eames Gallery in East Hampton, New York. According to the catalog:

> Any gentleman would prize David Ebner's elegant mahogany valet. Its bent, laminated, wishbone legs demonstrate his allegiance to both Wharton Esherick and his teacher, Wendell Castle.
>
> Pritam & Eames Gallery Archives

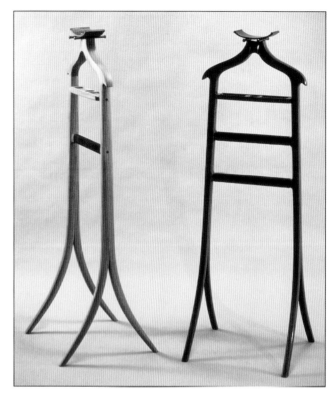

Two *Dressing Valets* of mahogany and clara walnut with ebony detail, 18″ d x 18″ w x 53″ h, 1993.

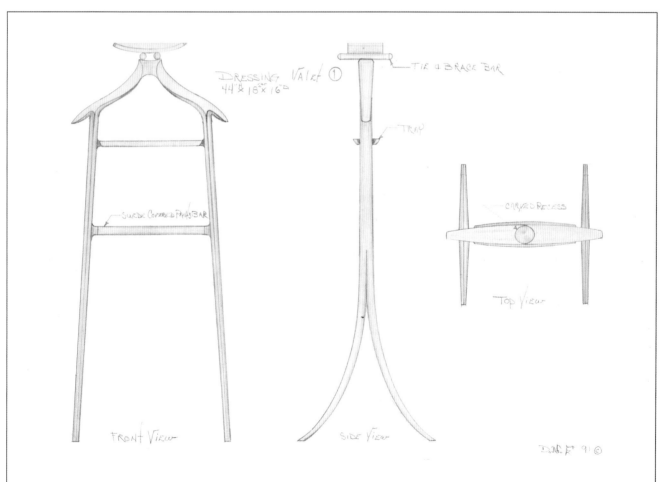

Dressing Valet, 1991.

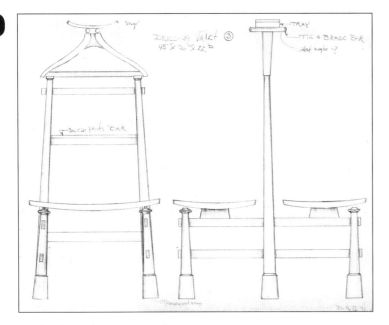

Another design for a *Dressing Valet*, 1991.

Dining Table or *Desk*, designed in 1992.

This extended table was commissioned to meet the owner's needs, in 1992. The top and base have peened brass surfaces, not a style usually associated with Ebner's work.

THE EBNER/BARNETT COLLABORATION

In 1992, an old friendship gave birth to a creative collaboration between David Ebner and Ivan Barnett. Documents in the Pritam & Eames Gallery Archives provide some background.

David Ebner and Ivan Barnett while they were working in collaboration, 1992 to 1995.

David Ebner and Ivan Barnett met as draftees during the Vietnam War period. They both ended up in an Army unit dedicated to display booth fabrication. Although Barnett went on to specialize in metal fabrication and jewelry, ...they stayed in touch. In the early 1990s, they decided to collaborate and produce a body of work designed with available parts made in production for other purposes. This included the bentwood parts that Mennonites used for wheels, steel harrow disks, and tool parts, particularly handles.

The oak and steel low table provided a particularly calligraphic announcement, but the favorite piece in the show was the stool. The dark tonalities of the painted finishes were a integral part of the theme, as was keeping most metal parts true to their industrial look.— Pritam & Eames Gallery Archives

In 1992, writer Barbara Delatiner wrote in *The New York Times*:

...the noted furniture maker [David Ebner]'s thoughts are frequently for the future. The signed and dated stools, chairs, chests and tables that he creates in his Bellport studio, he feels, are "the antiques of tomorrow." An exhibit of his pieces in collaboration with Ivan Barnett were exhibited at the Pritam & Eames Gallery of Original Furniture, in East Hampton, Long Island, New York. Mr. Barnett is a metal sculptor from Lancaster, Pennsylvania. Together "they make use of metal and painted finishes."... "Operating in what Mr. Barnett said was a 'Synergistic' fashion, the two got together and took different shapes, forms and materials and, 'juxtposing them,'... came up with 'assemblages – collages, if you like – of things that worked for us visually and were out of our customary mold.'"

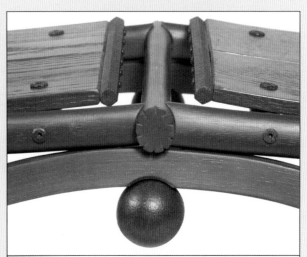

The steam-bent *Wagon-wheel Bench #1*, is from the Ebner/Barnett collaboration of 1992, in an edition of 12. Ash, oak, steel, gold leaf, with milk paint and graphite finishes, 16.5" d x 58" l x 18" h.

THE EBNER/BARNETT COLLABORATION

PHILOSOPHY AND POST-MODERN FURNITURE: THE EBNER/BARNETT COLLABORATION

The forms and shapes of tools derive from the system of uses to which they belong, each tool in the totality referring through its shape to the shape of all others. This was an insight of the philosopher Martin Heidegger and it is one of two philosophical concepts that help elucidate the aesthetics of the furniture works achieved through the collaboration of David Ebner and Ivan Barnett.

For *Heidegger*, a whole consisting of tools constitutes a kind of language, in which the tools imply one another throughout the system. One cannot understand the hammer without knowledge of the nail, not to mention the nail without seeing the way it refers to wood. Consider, since it plays a considerable role in certain of the Ebner/Barnett pieces, the handle of the axe. It refers at one of its extremities to the grip of human hands, and, at the other, to the blade. Human beings in fact form temporary parts of the tool system in which axes figure, for the handle of the axe draws an implicit picture of what a person must do in order that the axe be properly used. The axe must be *swung* by someone standing erect, with spread legs, and the handle's elegant curvatures is a portrait of the true swing. The axe cannot be as slender where the woodman grasps it as it is at mid-shaft; its other extremity must be just thick enough to hold the blade without taking more of the blade's mass than necessary. The handle is a portrait of lightness, strength, and power, and its length must be exactly suited to human reality and instrumental effectiveness. This explains the aesthetics of the axe handle, when we contemplate it on its own, and outside the system in which its form evolved. That form is a memory of its use.

The other philosophical concept derives from the writing of *Claude Levi-Strauss* on the mentality of primitive peoples. The primitive fits things together which do not belong to the same tool-system, but which somehow or other work together in their new conjunction. His procedures are impulsive and intuitive rather than rational and calculated. This art of assembling discordant elements into new wholes *Levi-Strauss* designates *bricolage*, a French word which refers to the way someone improves novel situations, using whatever is at hand. Ebner/Barnett's use of axe handles to form the stretchers of tables, and mounting them on half circles taken from the system of the wheelwright, is as good an example of *bricolage* as can be imagined. The axe handles retain the poetry of their use, as this is inscribed in their form, but are given place in a work of art where their function is transformed into beauty. They are like a piece of familiar poetry embedded in a fresh poem, alluding to the one context and vitalizing the other through allusion and association.

I have used the slash-sign in Ebner/Barnett, rather than a sign for conjunction, to underscore, graphically, that these works are collaborative in inspiration, and in realization. Collaboration in art today takes a stand against the image of the solitary creative ego that has defined our image of the artist since the age of Romanticism. In collaborating, it is the collaborative that creates, a *we* rather than an *I*: the selves are somehow transcended to form a new kind of person. The collaborative relationship is being found more and more in the art world today. But the objects of *this* Ebner/Barnett collaboration too belong to this special moment in art history, through their appropriation, into novel wholes, of elements and components wrenched from the tool systems that first gave them their life and form. The furniture, like the collaborative spirit it embodies, belongs to the post-modern moment.

It seems somehow suitable, if *bricolage* expresses the primitive spirit, that these remarkable works, assembled out of elements from the modern world, should seem to convey the power and authority of tribal objects— of chieftain's stools, of altars, of tables for ritual enactments.

—Arthur C. Danto
1993
The Johnsonian Professor of Philosophy at
Columbia University and art critic of *The Nation*

Mirror #1 made during the collaboration of David Ebner and Ivan Barnett, 1992-95, with pumpkin-colored milk paint, blued steel, and woven silver wire details, 33" w x 3" d x 21" h.

Table Lamp #3, 1994, made during the Ebner/Bartlett collaboration, 28" h, with a handmade paper shade, 16" d.

THE EBNER/BARNETT COLLABORATION

Table lamp, c. 1994, made during the Ebner/Bartlett collaboration, 28" h.

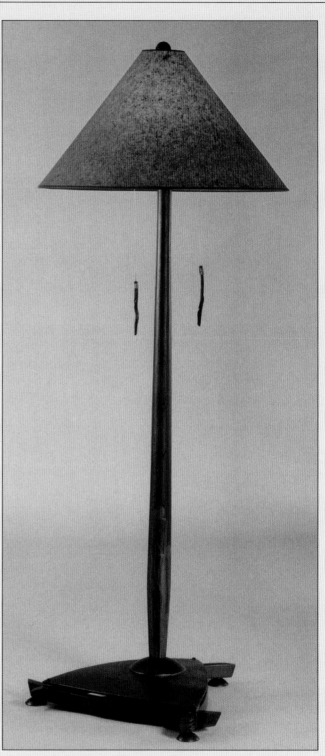

Floor Lamp #4, 1994, made during the Ebner/Barnett collaboration, hickory, steel, graphite, milk paint, 24" w x 58" h, with a polychrome, handmade, paper shade, 24" d.

Mirror #2 made during the Ebner/Barnett collaboration, 1992-95, with a milk-painted shelf and bronze details, 33″ w x 7″ d x 25″ h.

Table lamp, made during the Ebner/Barnett collaboration in 1994, steel, 27″ w x 9″ d x 22″ h.

THE EBNER/BARNETT COLLABORATION

Table #5 on three legs, made during the Ebner/ Barnett collaboration, 1992-93, with a leather top, milk paint, a graphite finish, and bronze details, 37" w x 37" d x 32" h.

In late 1993, the Edith Lambert Gallery, on Canyon Road, in Santa Fe, New Mexico, held an exhibit of the furniture made in collaboration by David Ebner and Ivan Barnett. Dean Balsamo, reviewing the exhibit for the *Sante Fe New Mexican*, wrote:

> The tables and stools radiate strength and a no-nonsense approach. The latter is highlighted by the subtle way they achieve their innovative designs. The colors are muted and decoration is used to feed the overall tone of the work, not call attention to itself. Ebner and Barnett's works are reflections of artists who allow their individual egos to serve a greater whole.
>
> "Gallery Hopping,"
> *The Santa Fe New Mexican*,
> December 10, 1993

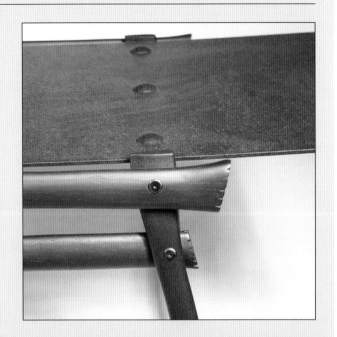

Coffee Table, with rusted metal top and axe-handle-shaped legs and stretchers, part of the Ebner/Barnett collaboration, 1992-94, 48" w x 28" d x 16" h.

THE EBNER/BARNETT COLLABORATION

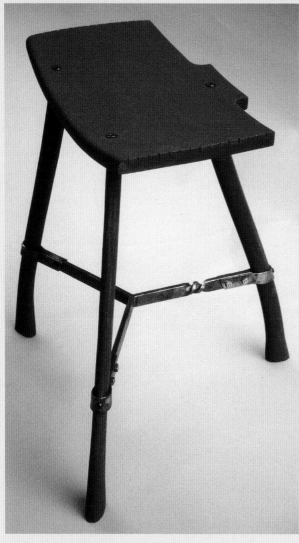

This *Three-legged Stool* is part of the Barnett/Ebner collaboration, with axe handles, a chair seat, and forged steel detail, c. 1992, 20" w x 12" d x 25" h.

Alice Webb wrote of this exhibit in *The Magazine Antiques*, January/February 1994:

> Ash, hickory and oak blend with bronze and steel to form the body of the pieces, while nuts and bolts unabashedly pin rungs and are counterbalanced by touches of gold leaf. ...Delightfully confusing the mind, Barnett/Ebner shape and stain wood soft blacks and dark greens so that it appears like metal, and conversely the metal is textured to look like wood. This *trompe l'oeil* technique made clarification of the difference discernible only by touching and thumping the various parts, the legs, the tabletops.

In the fall of 1995, Ebner and Barnett showed works at the Pritam & Eames Gallery.

> In this fall exhibit, a group of table lamps and a floor standing lamp ...continued Ebner and Barnett's exploration of combining pre-existing industrial parts within the craft process.

Pritam & Eames Archives

Stool made during the Ebner/Barnett collaboration of blued steel, steamed white oak and maple, and gold-leaf balls underneath, 11" d x 23" w x 19" h.

Table made during the Ebner/Barnett collaboration, in 1993, with a rusted metal shelf and tubular metal supports for an oval glass top, 1992, 50" w x 28" d x 17" h.

THE EBNER/BARNETT COLLABORATION

Ebner gave some insight into how the collaboration worked in a 1996 interview with Chuck Anderson, which appeared in the *Long Island Advance*:

> "We're doing a series of furniture and decorative objects," said Ebner. "It's a new direction for us. We design and execute a piece together, then I take over its fabrication. Once the piece is made, Ivan takes over, finishing and painting its surface. He also takes care of the marketing. Our wood sculptures are based on Native American sand painting, which has religious connotations."
>
> "David Ebner, craftsman and artist," *The Long Island Advance*, September 26, 1996.

Console Table #4, made during the Ebner/Barnett collaboration, in 1993, in an edition of eight. It has a peaned bronze top and wood and metal base. Bronze, brass, steel, hickory, ash, 60" l x 17.5" d x 26.5" h.

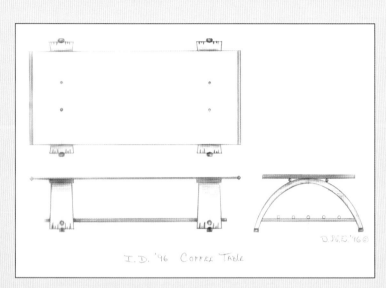

Drawing of a *Coffee Table,* 1996.

Coffee table of oak and steel, made during the Ebner/Barnett collaboration, in 1995, 48″ w x 22″ d x 14″ h.

THE EBNER/BARNETT COLLABORATION

Two-seat Bench made with ash, maple, brass, and leather, during the Ebner/Barnett collaboration, 1993-95, 60" w x 15" d x 20" h.

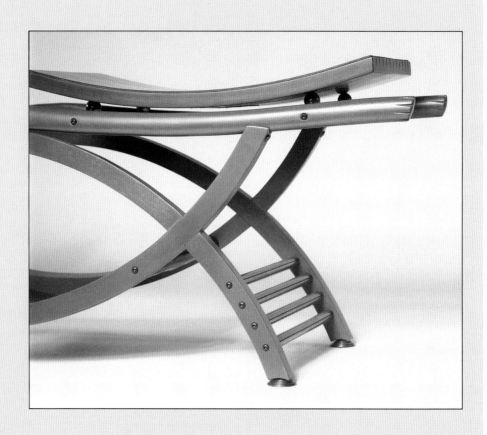

Entertainment Center, with a motorized, pop-up shelf section in a rift red oak veneered case with gunmetal trim. 24″ d x 60″w x 38″ h.

Gallery North, at Setauket, New York, staged a joint show of Joseph Reboli's paintings and David Ebner's elegant and classical new furniture in October, 1995.

Shown were Ebner's occasional chair in ribbon mahogany with wenge detail, mahogany end tables, a rocking chair—barrel backed, of red oak, cane, and exquisite proportions, and a ribbon mahogany writing desk.

Reviewing the show for the *Three Village Herald*, Susan Bridson stated, " ...you have to see these graceful lines and gorgeous woods to appreciate what he has achieved." She continued:

> More frolicsome are his ladder chair of sassafras and rush, the pair of four-foot-tall sassafras and blued steel candlesticks, and the ladder-back chair of curly maple. Mr. Ebner's genius blazes in this show, most particularly in the writing desk with its hint of fluid cyma curves, its superb dimensions, and beautiful satinwood inlay. This, truly, is sculpture in wood.
>
> "Stunning show at gallery," *The Three Village Herald* October 4, 1995.

Two *Wall Sconces*, 1994, with handmade paper light diffusers and frames of oak, afromosia, walnut and wenge, 9″ w x 5″ d x 18″ h.

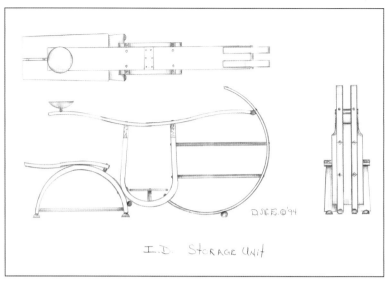

Drawing of a *Storage Chest*, 1994

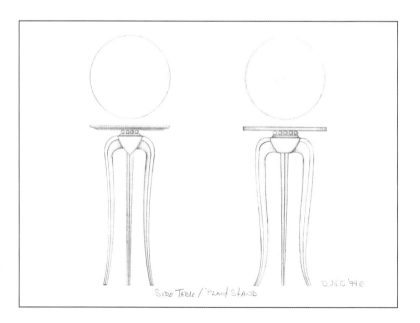

Drawing of a *Side Table* or *Plant Stand*, 1994.

A unique *Cabinet* of pomaré sapele, with glass panes and brass knobs on the hinged doors, 1998, 40″ w x 16″ d x 50″ h.

Slatted Bench (designed before the bamboo one), in afromosia wood, 1998, 44″ w x 15″ d x 20″ h.

In 2000, Ebner participated in the exhibit *2000 & Ten* at the Pritam & Eames Gallery, along with nine other artists.

There was the solid afromosia bench by David Ebner with its swayed, slatted seat and comfortable pillowed wood arms.
— *Pritam & Eames Archives*

In the winter of 2000, he completed a set of fireplace tools and stand, in sassafras, brass and steel.

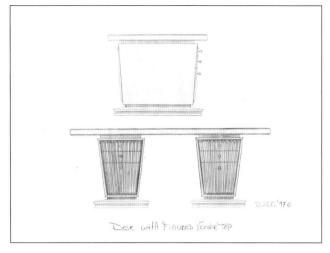

Drawing of a *Desk* with figured veneer top, 1997

Drawing of a *Console Table* or *Desk*, showing details of various foot designs, 1997.

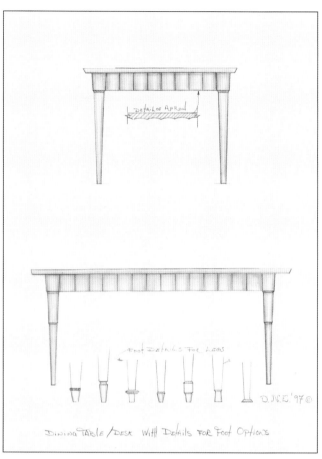

Console Table or *Desk* with a scalloped edge, rectangular top of pomaré sapele and four curved legs, 1998, 72" w x 20" d x 32" h.

Console Table or *Desk* with a scalloped edge, rectangular top of pomaré sapele and four curved legs, 1998, 72″ w x 20″ d x 32″ h.

SCREWBALL BAT

In 1997, Craig Nutt, a wood turner and furniture maker from Tennessee, curated an exhibit at the Kentucky Arts and Crafts Gallery, entitled "Bats & Bowls." The touring exhibit began in Louisville, home of the Louisville Slugger, from May 14 to July 5, 1997.

Nutt described the concept behind the exhibit in the catalog:

> The art of wood turning has much in common with the game of baseball. Imagine the batter stepping up to the plate, the wood turner approaching the lathe, each seeking the precise balance between freedom and stability. The ball player's bat and the turner's gouge become extensions of the body, each seeking the sweet spot of the object spinning toward it. Both the player and the turner are focused on results yet fully involved with the process. Each pursuit has its own sense of time. They are linked by a turned object, the baseball bat.
>
> The artists in this exhibition were invited to create a bat, either from an ash blank provided by Hillerich & Bradsby Co., or from materials of the artist's choice. In addition, each artist was asked to exhibit a work with is representative of his or her body of work.
>
> [The exhibit provided] a fresh and creative look at the implement which is at the heart of the national pastime, the bat—and a glimpse into the world of artists who exemplify the art of turning.

Ebner must have felt like he was returning to his youth and early work as he exhibited unique turnings as baseball bat designs.

During October 1997, David Ebner had an important exhibit at Gallery North, in Setauket, New York. The bats were included and found their way into a review by Helen A. Harrison:

> Mr. Ebner's goofy baseball bats made of exotic woods combine technical finesse with humor, adding a twist, both literal and figurative. The "Screwball Bat" sports a spiral shaft, while "Ball in Bat" seems to have swallowed its target and got indigestion in the process. Twisted, warped or wavy, one of Mr. Ebner's bats would be (forgive the pun) the hit of any baseball fan's collection
>
> "ART; Some Luminous Surfaces and
> 2 Asian Survey Shows,"
> *The New York Times*, Long Island edition
> October 12, 1997.

1985–2004

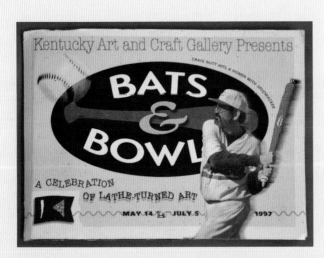

An ebonized ash *Screwball Bat* was first shown in the "Bat & Bowl" show at the Kentucky Art and Craft Gallery's "Celebration of Lathe Turned Art," 1997. Ebner recalls:

> That was done for the inaugural show at the Louisville Slugger Museum. They picked about eighteen woodworkers who did turning and sent them billets of ash and asked us to make a contemporary expression in a bat. I made a screwball bat. I made the bat look like a big screw, in reference to a screwball. There were a lot of different approaches used, but that's what I did.

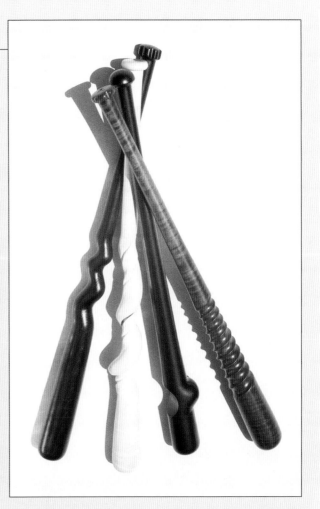

This *Coffee Table* has a free-form, elm burl, plank top with quartered sycamore medallions, and peaned and blued steel detail on two round side supports and straight horizontal feet, 1999, 47" w x 30" d x 17" h.

Slab Dining Table in quartered sycamore with a natural edge, 1998, 72" l x 28" w x 30" h.

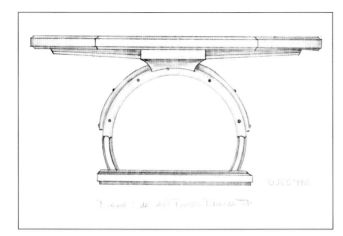

Drawing of a dining table with a peened bronze top, 1999, and as made with a wood top.

Drawing for *Bench 2*, 1999.

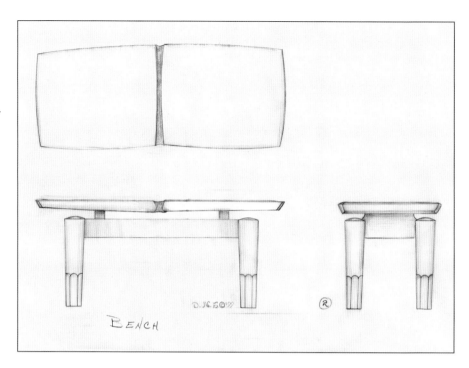

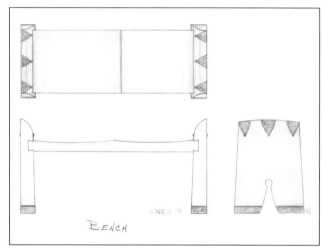

Drawing for *Bench 6*, 1999.

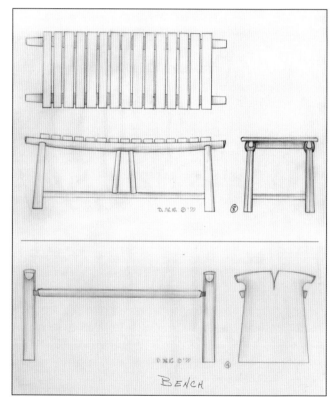

Drawing for *Bench 8* and *Bench 4*

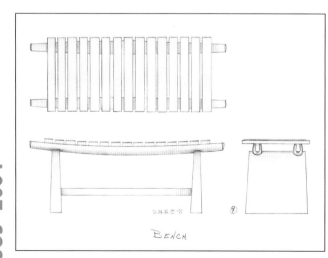

Drawing for *Bench 7*, 1999.

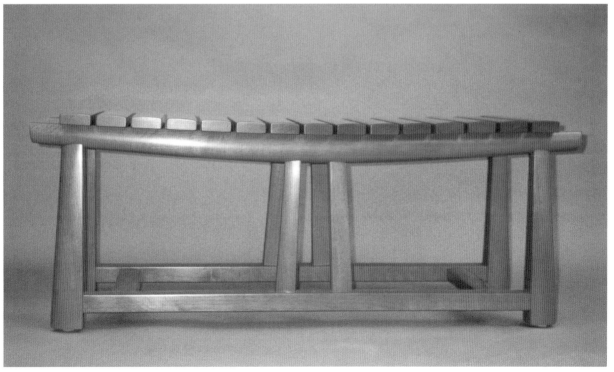

Plank Bench, Bench 8, of Spanish cedar, 1999.

BAMBOO SERIES

David Ebner had been fascinated by the strength and laminating potential of bamboo for a long time. Writing in 2008, Jonathan Binzin reports:

Bamboo intrigued him, but he couldn't see how he might incorporate it in his furniture. The connection didn't come clear, in fact, until 20 years later, when bamboo sheet goods—made from bamboo cut into strips and then glued together—appeared on the market. At that point, he says, "I finally had the raw material to go along with the vocabulary of my Asian-inspired designs."

Binzen, Op.cit., page 20

Ebner had worked with various forms of bamboo, casually, until 2002, when it became more available commercially and he devoted a concentrated period to refine his techniques to shape it.

Ebner recalls his history with this material:

I waited many years to get involved [with bamboo] because when I first started thinking about working in bamboo, the raw material wasn't available, other than naturally grown bamboo. Eventually, because of market demand and in the spirit of green energy, the bamboo industry blossomed in the last ten years to where cheap goods are available. That's what allowed me to get involved in doing a series of bamboo pieces.

The idea of being really simple was very important to me, kind of an acknowledgement to the culture and how the Asians would build things, with the pure use of the material. All these pieces were done with the minimal components. A lot of the designs were inspired by Japanese calligraphy and the written word, which I have a book about that I bought thirty years ago.

It was a chance to combine things after a long period of time waiting for the raw material. I've done a lot with the vacuum pressing and tapered panels to allow me to have these soft, graceful lines.

A sideboard was the first bamboo piece made. Flooring material was the first sheets of bamboo available to work with; they were sanded down to create the thin strips needed for the furniture. Then, veneers of bamboo became available in the market place.

Binzin strikes similar themes in his assessment of Ebner's bamboo work:

In designing his current line of pieces in bamboo, he drew on elements of simplicity and economy that he had admired in Chinese calligraphy. He saw that in calligraphy each line mattered immensely. Attempting to create furniture with the fewest possible lines led him to design in planes instead of sticks and to taper the thickness of some of the planes—like the legs on his bench—so that from the edge they might recall the tapering stroke from a calligrapher's brush.

Binzen, Op.cit., page 20

Ebner shared his thoughts about his work with bamboo, in his 2004 catalog entitled *Signed Editions*:

These pieces in bamboo mark the beginning of a whole new direction for me. I started experimenting with bamboo veneer and laminated sheet goods three years ago, learning how to work with its inherent qualities. One of the reasons I am drawn to bamboo, beside its natural beauty, is that it could possibly be the quintessential replenishable building materials known to man. I find that I have to constantly remind myself that bamboo is a grass and not a wood. Other pieces planned for this series are a piano bench, bed, and blanket chest.

Occasional Table, part of
the Bamboo Series, 2002.

BAMBOO SERIES

Bench in the Bamboo Series,
42″ w x 14″ d x 16.5″ w.

This bamboo *Serving Tray* of
rectangular shape has raised sides
and two raised handles at the
short ends, 2002, 22″ w x 13″ d x
3.5″ h.

Table of bamboo with a
stretcher base.

Sideboard or *Console Table*, 2002, bamboo. This table was the first in a series of designs based on simplicity derived from calligraphy, 33″ h x 15″ d x 45″ w.

BAMBOO SERIES

Counter Stool in amber bamboo, 2007, 16.5" w x 13" d x 25" h.

Small Stool in layered bamboo with a metal stretcher, 17" w x 13" d x 17" h.

A small *End Table* of bamboo with a rectangular, two-piece top and four, gently flaring, turned legs. The design was inspired by Japanese tora gates and first made in rosewood and ebony in the early 1980s; this table was made in 2003, 14" w x 24" d x 24" h.

BAMBOO SERIES

Slatted Bench, 2004, bamboo with bronze details, 2004, 22″ h x 15″ d x 44″ w.

Vanity or piano bench of bamboo with bronze detail and calf hide seat, 2004, 30″ w x 15″ d x 18″ h.

Dome-topped *funa chest* of bamboo with a hinged lid and curved sides resting on two straight feet. A metal escutcheon and side pulls are attachments. This was the last of the bamboo series designs, with some construction techniques based on old Chinese styles brought up to date, not just as ornament, 35.5" w x 28" d x 20" h.

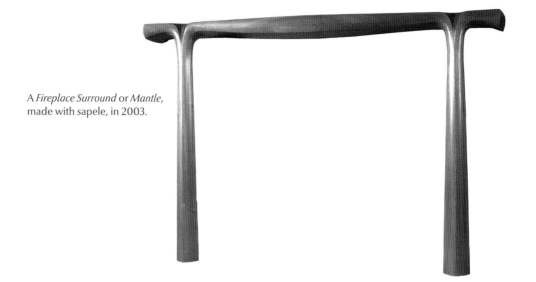

A *Fireplace Surround* or *Mantle*,
made with sapele, in 2003.

Chest of Drawers, 2003. The updated
version of this early design was made
in two variations: figured white ash
and quartered sapele. Originally
designed in 1965, when David Ebner
was a sophomore at the Rochester
Institute of Technology, the chest has
been made at various times during his
career. Ebner comments:

We talk about how sometimes
artists will revisit early
themes; thirty years later I
revisited this chest design,
and I changed it. The size
is the same, the spirit is the
same, I just changed the lines
on it to catch up to how I am
drawing and designing today. I
do revisit themes, and if I like
the essence, sometimes I will
leave it alone, but on this piece,
I made some pretty significant
changes that I felt brought it
into a more total design, more
successful for me.

That has to do with revisiting
work, and I think the older
you get the more you tend
to look back and like to
capture those moments of
pure inspiration. Sometimes
I think we get cluttered with
some many ideas, so many
directions, it's nice to revisit
early work, when you're so
pure and focused and un-
distracted.

BRONZE SIGNED EDITIONS

The casting of David Ebner's furniture designs in bronze was an idea he had carried around for a number of years.

> There was a point when I decided I wanted to do some of my pieces in bronze. I never actually designed a piece specifically for bronze; I revisited my portfolio and picked the pieces that would have a voice in bronze. I like the idea that bronze is going to last a lot longer than wood; you know these pieces are going to be around for a long time. It appealed to a different market. Some people buy bronze, they don't look at wood; it actually expanded the potential for marketing. I really wanted to see some of my objects in bronze. That scallion is pretty attractive in bronze and has a great presence.

Ebner's cast bronze *Scallion Coat Rack* and his cast bronze *Renwick Stool* were exhibited in 2001.

Beebe Johnson is a co-founder of the Pritam & Eames Gallery, in East Hampton, New York, which has hosted many exhibits of David Ebner's work over the years. She explained how David Ebner's bronze signed editions came about. These pieces were all executed at the Mussi Artworks Foundry in Berkeley, California.

> Working with the artisans at Mussi Artworks Foundry in California, David Ebner has recreated some of his classic wood pieces in bronze. This new body of bronze work displays both a certainty borne of experience and a maturity of artistic vision.
>
> Wood has been his principal medium, as many of the forms that influenced him are found in pieces inspired by the work of Wharton Esherick. Ebner has made chairs and tables that evoke the beauty of extended branches, sometimes using wood that has been twisted and shaped by honeysuckle. His *Scallion Hat Rack*, *Bench*, and *Twisted Stick Candlesticks*, now available in a new bronze edition series, are classic Ebner pieces that satisfy us as both sculpture and as art. Other signature pieces in the bronze series include his classical *Renwick Stool*, named for the stool in wood original, that is in the permanent collection of the Smithsonian Institution's Museum of American Art, in Washington, D.C.

An early *Renwick Bench*, designed in 1974, was the first of two sand castings, in bronze and in aluminum, 2003, 16" w x 15" d x 16.5" h.

BRONZE SIGNED EDITIONS

Museum of Fine Arts (MFA) Bench, 2001, Honduras mahogany and made in painted wood, 15"h x 16" d x 38"w. Made in cast bronze and finished with a variety of patinas, 2003, in an edition of fifteen, 17" h x 15.5" d x 36" w.

Scallion Coat Rack, cast bronze, 19″ w x 12″ d x 69″ h.

BRONZE SIGNED EDITIONS

Vessel I, cast bronze, 13" w x 12" d x 2.5" h.

Corner Table, cast bronze,
24" w x 18" d x 30.5" h.

Vessel II, cast bronze, 15" w x 12" d x 3.5" h.

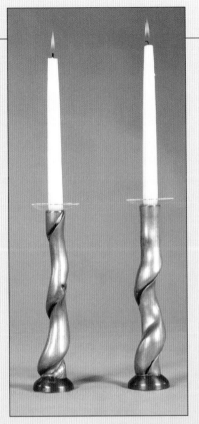

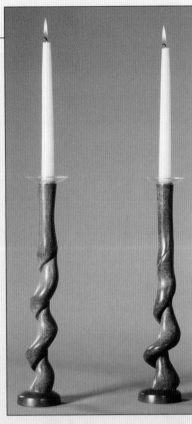

Far left:
Candle Holders I, from the "Twisted-sticks" designs, cast bronze, 2.5" d x 10.5" h.

Left:
Candle Holders II, from the "Twisted-sticks" designs, cast bronze, 3" d x 15" h.

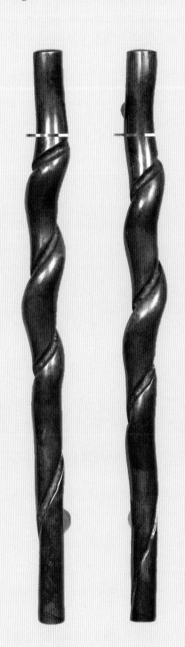

Door Pulls, from the "Twisted-sticks" designs, cast bronze in two sizes: 2.5" d x 16" h and 3.5" d x 23" h.

CHAPTER 5
BROOKHAVEN STUDIO
2004–2013

David Ebner carving in
the Brookhaven Studio.

David Ebner views his current studio
as both a place of solitude and a sanctuary,
where he seeks and learns new ways to
express himself in furniture forms.

The fourth, and current, studio in Brookhaven,
New York, 2004–present.

In the last decade, Ebner has both revisited his earlier designs with variations in new materials and also struck out to find new shapes to add to his portfolio. It is a never-ending process of renewal and adventure for him. As commissions come in from old and new admirers, he explores the possibilities of realizing designs to suit the needs of his customers and his own curiosity. His older work has become sought-after and his new work attracts attention.

Foyer Table, ash, commissioned in 2004.

A Bedroom Suite of matching lacewood furniture, 2006. The set includes:

- *Double Chest* of six drawers, with two bail pulls on each drawer and a rectangular top.
- *Double Chest* of six drawers, with a single bail pull on each drawer.
- *Sink Vanity Cabinet* with a single drawer, a stack of three drawers, and two doors.

Black Wave Table with a slate top,
peened and blued steel base,
with a graphited lacquered finish,
2009, 20" w x 18" d x 22" h.

Stacked, figured ash *Coffee Table* with an oval, book-matched, plank top and a laminated, oval base, 2008, 72" w x 42" d x 16" h.

Library Steps, walnut, 49" h x 19" w x 22" d, 2009. This design was made after the *Writing Chair* that had been in his sketch book for about fifteen years. The Wharton Esherick Museum had a competition of library steps in 2009, so this was constructed then. It has been a successful design.

The recent tables are good examples of Ebner trying to use his figured woods more economically by making up veneers. He made the veneers for them, giving him a great bookmatch for the tops and sides. He adds:

> This was probably a board left over from the bedroom commission which I'm doing much more consciously now, taking my figured woods and making them into veneers.

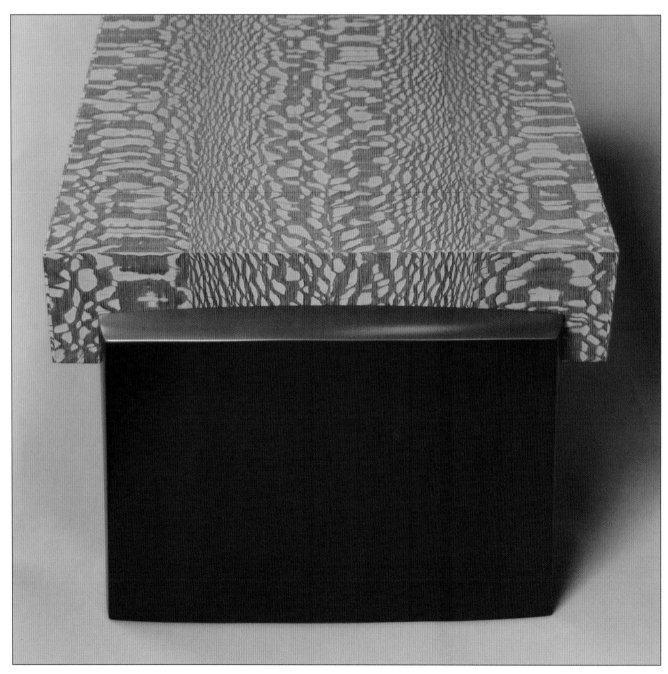

Coffee Table with a highly-figured, book-matched, Australian lacewood veneered op and a shelf, supported with graphite-finished maple supports, 2010.

Rectangular *Dining Table* with a highly figured elm burl, two-board top, and four English brown oak, gently curved legs, 2010.

Console Table, c. 2012, zebra wood with hand-cast bronze pulls, 48″ w x 16″ d x 26″ h.

Lacewood foyer table, 2012.

Round Dining Table of ovangkol, 55" w x 30" h. A unique feature of this *Table* is the inlaid, fan pattern of the overhanging, circular top. This table, made in 2012, has a floating top that was veneered in a vacuum bag. David Ebner is making his own veneers to keep the wood stable. The leg is dovetailed into its laminated skirt, so that no stretcher is needed.

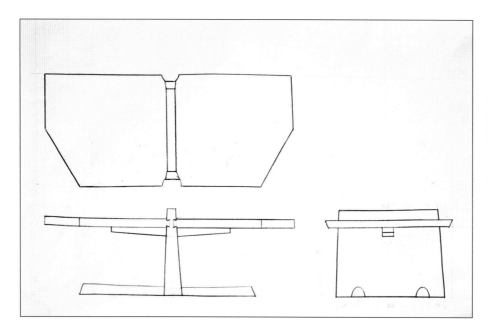

Construction drawing and the *Kahn Coffee Table,* made from walnut and quartered sycamore. A tapered dovetail slips into a joint, where the flat top meets the central support, 2013, 50″ w x 25″ d x 19″ h.

End Table of elm burl with a bronzing powdered, lacquered base, 2012, 22″ w x 15″ d x 22″ h.

Coffee table with an elm burl top and wenge and afromosia base, 2013, 42″ w x 36″ d x 17″ h.

MFA Bench in burnished, blue, milk paint over maple, made for the competition "Poplar Culture," at the Wharton Esherick Museum, in Paoli, Pennsylvania, for the celebration of a tree at the museum, 2012.

Desk/Dining Table, with a book-matched teak top and brushed stainless steel base, 84" l x 40" w x 30" h.

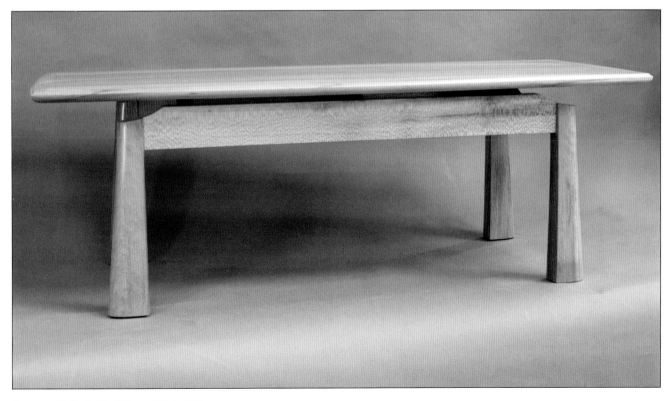

Sycamore Coffee Table, 60" w x 20" d x 17" h.

ARCHITECTURAL DRAWINGS FOR PROPOSED STUDIO RENOVATIONS

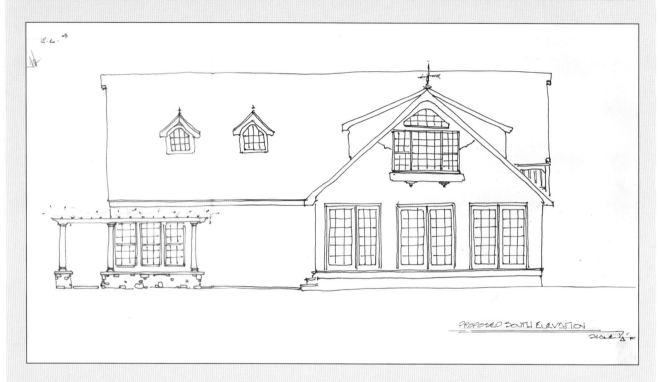

PROPOSED SOUTH ELEVATION

PROP WEST ELEVATION-DAVID N. EBNER STUDIO

Two architectural drawings, for proposed studio renovations, were developed by Greg Schroth.

AFTERWORD

David Ebner is on the cutting edge of designing and producing new modes of studio craft furniture that are fast becoming the definitive model of contemporary American art. In 1991, John Perreault made the connection between Ebner and the other great twentieth century furniture artists. What he wrote the is still cogent today:

> Through the use of stripped-down classic forms, David Ebner has updated and extended the mode of furniture solidified by Wharton Esherick, George Nakashima, Sam Maloof, and the early Wendell Castle, quietly establishing himself as a designer-craftsman (his term) capable of producing functional art that is practical, relatively affordable, and likely to endure. Although he does make unique pieces —on speculation, on commission, or because the wood he is using or the style he is analyzing demands this, as is the case with the new, twisted-stick furniture—the major concentration of his art-making, excepting his turned bowls, is in the realm of studio production. This distances him somewhat from his distinguished predecessors and, at the same time, creates an aesthetic edge: Handmade furniture as art, he seems to be saying, does not have to be one-of-a kind or custom-made.—
>
> Perreault, *Op.cit.*, page 15

As Ebner himself has said,

> Decorative art is what it is. I'm taking studio art to another step without just being a reproducing craftsman…. I think of it as taking things from history for history, as the antiques of tomorrow.
>
> Cromeyn, *Op.cit.*

TIMELINE

SELECTED EVENTS FOR DAVID N. EBNER

1945 • Born in Buffalo, New York

1964 • High School Diploma from Kenmore East High School, Buffalo, New York

1968 • Bachelor of Fine Arts degree from The School for American Craftsmen at Rochester Institute of Technology, Rochester, New York

1969 • Studies at the London School of Furniture Design and Production, London, England

1969–1971 • U.S. Army service in Washington, D. C.

1971–1973 • Travels in the United States

1973 • Establishes his first studio in a garage at Blue Point, on the south shore of Long Island, New York State

1975 • Exhibits at "Craft Multiples" show at the Renwick Gallery, Washington, D. C., July 4, 1975 –February 16, 1976 and circulating in the United States from March 1976 through March 1979.

1976 • Establishes his second studio in a barn at Brookhaven Hamlet, New York
• Scallions series begun

1984 • May 5–June 17, exhibit "Master Furniture Makers of the '80s," Gallery Henoch, New York, New York

1985 • Establishes his third studio in Bellport, New York, in a building owned by the Bellport Historical Society

1988 • Earned American Craft Award from The Guild Publishing, Madison, Wisconsin

1990 • July 15–August 7, exhibits at "Lathe-turned Furniture" at Ten Arrow Gallery, Cambridge, Massachusetts
• Exhibited at "Sitting Pretty," at Pritam & Eames Gallery, East Hampton, New York

1991 • May 9–August 4, exhibited at "Explorations II, The New Furniture," at The American Craft Museum, New York, New York
• May 17-August 4, exhibit "International Lathe-turned Objects Challenge IV," at the Port of History Museum, Philadelphia, Pennsylvania and touring the United States through April 12, 1992
• November to January, 1992, Exhibit "New Work" at Pritam & Eames Gallery, East Hampton, New York

1992 • Exhibit "Early Spring Show" at Pritam & Eames Gallery, East Hampton, New York

1992-1994 • "Collaboration" furniture with Ivan Barnett

1993 • December, exhibits furniture at the Edith Lambert Gallery, Canyon Road, Santa Fe, New Mexico.

1997 • May 14–July 5, exhibits at "Bats & Bowls, A Celebration of Lathe-turned Art" at the Kentucky Arts and Crafts Gallery, Louisville

2001 • September 29–January 13, 2002, exhibit The Chair Show 4, Asheville, North Carolina: Southern Highland Craft Guild.

2002 • October 12–November 23, Exhibit "The Chair," Worcester Center for Crafts, Krikorian Gallery, curated by Sam Maloof

2003 ◆ Learns bronze casting and creates bronze signed editions of some of his wood pieces at Mussi Artworks Foundry in California

2004 ◆ Establishes his fourth studio at Brookhaven, New York

2005 ◆ July 1–August 9, Exhibits at Pritam & Eames Gallery, East Hampton, New York, featuring new work in bamboo

2008 ◆ June 19–July 17, Exhibits in "Seats of New York: Benches, Stools & Chairs from Across the State," at the Richard & Dolly Maass Gallery, Purchase, New York, Sponsored by The Furniture Society

2009 ◆ May 22-June 30, Exhibits at "The Case for Carving," Pritam & Eames Gallery, East Hampton, New York

2010 ◆ Review of art of the studio craft furniture movement cites Ebner as creating "the antiques of tomorrow"

2013 ◆ June 28–September 28, Exhibit "Material, Process and Form, The Furniture of David Ebner," at Suffolk County Historical Society, Riverhead, New York

SELECTED EXHIBITIONS

National Collection of Fine Arts, Smithsonian Institution, Washington, D.C.
"Exploration II, The New Furniture," American Crafts Museum, New York, NY
"Bed and Board," Decordova Museum, Lincoln, Massachusetts
Guild Hall Museum, East Hampton, NY
"A Decade of Crafts: Recent Acquisitions," American Crafts Museum, New York, NY

Gallery Fair, Mendocino, CA
Pritam & Eames Gallery, East Hampton, NY
"The Chair," The Worcester Center for Crafts, Art Basel, Switzerland
SOFA: New York, Chicago, Santa Fe

SELECTED COLLECTIONS

American Craft Museum, New York, NY
The Art Institute of Chicago, Chicago, IL
Baylar Art Museum, University of Virginia, Charlottesville, VA
Glenn Close, New York, NY
Tony Delorenzo, New York, NY
William & Elaine de Kooning, East Hampton, NY
Forbes Magazine Collection, New York, NY
Gerald D. Hines, Dallas TX
High Museum, Atlanta, Georgia
Horace Havemeyer III, New York, NY
Isabella Rossellini, Bellport, NY
Lord & Lady de Rothschild, London, England
Museum of Fine Arts, Boston, MA
National Collection of Fine Art, Smithsonian Institution, Washington, D.C.
Yale University Art Gallery, New Haven, CT.

SELECTED PUBLICATIONS

The New York Times
American Craft
Fine Woodworking
House and Garden
Newsday
Art and Crafts International
Garden Magazine
Art & Antiques

BIBLIOGRAPHY

Anderson, Chuck. "David Ebner, craftsman and artist," The Long Island Advance, September 26, 1996.

Balsamo, Dean. "Gallery Hopping," *The Santa Fe New Mexican*, December 10, 1993.

Berg, Janet. "Antiques of the Future, Bellport Artist David Ebner Imitates Natural Forms to Create Furniture," *Dan's Papers*, January 30, 1998.

Binzin, Jonathan. *Seats of New York: Benches, Stools, & Chairs from Across the State*, June 19–July 17, 2008, Purchase, New York: Richard & Dolly Maass Gallery, Purchase College, SUNY, 2008.

Bridson, Susan. "Stunning show at gallery," *The Three Village Herald*. October 4, 1995.

Craft Multiples, Washington, D.C.: Smithsonian Institution Press, 1975.

Cromeyn, Chris. "Bellport artisan on…The Cutting Edge," *The Long Island Advance*, June 3, 1999, page 11.

Danto, Arthur C. "Philosophy and Post-modern Furniture: The Ebner/Barnett Collaboration." Essay and letter dated September 2, 1993, in the possession of David Ebner.

Delatiner, Barbara. "A Creator of 'Antiques of Tomorrow.' *The New York Times*, Long Island edition, July 5, 1992, page 10.

Fitzgerald, Oscar P., *Studio Furniture of the Renwick Gallery Smithsonian American Art Museum*. Washington, D.C.: Smithsonian American Art museum.

Harrison, Helen A. "Crafts and Art: Do They Differ?", Long Island Weekly Magazine, *The New York Times*. October 11, 1981.

————. "Objects that Combine Practicality with Beauty," *The New York Times*, Long Island edition, page 17, July 1, 1979.

————. "ART; Some Luminous Surfaces And 2 Asian Survey Shows," *The New York Times*, Long Island edition, October 12, 1997.

Kartalis, Betty. "Breaking the Barrier between Craftsman and Artist," *Shore Lines*, June, 1986.

Landis, Scott, editor. *Conservation by Design*.Providence: Museum of Art, Rhode island School of Design, 1993.

Long, Robert. "Exquisite Artistry of Crafts in Guild Hall Exhibition," *Southampton Press*, December 21, 1989.

Louie, Elaine. "Furniture as Art: Shape and Symbol." *The New York Times*, May 9, 1991.

Main, Kari M. *Please Be Seated, Contemporary Studio Seating Furniture*. New Haven: Yale University Art Gallery, 1999.

Perreault, John. Exhibit catalog, "Explorations II, The New Furniture," New York City: The American Craft Museum, 1991.

Rosenberg, Maxine B. *Artists of Handcrafted Furniture at Work*. New York: Lothrop, Lee & Shepard Books.

Temin, Christine. "Lathe Works Star In Furniture Show," *Boston Globe*, February 1, 1990.

Tyler, Jan. "The Bellport Bench, Classic Village Charm Interpreted in a Contemporary Way," *The New York Times*, July, 1990.

Webb, Alice. *The Magazine Antiques*, January/February, 1994.

Wood Turning Center, Inc. *International Lathe-turned Objects, Challenge IV*. Philadelphia: Wood Turning Center, Inc., 1991.

INDEX